The Gardens
at Brantwood

The Gardens at Brantwood

Evolution of John Ruskin's Lakeland paradise

David Ingram

PALLAS ATHENE
& THE RUSKIN FOUNDATION

Opposite title page: Red-leaved Japanese Maples in spring, their gnarled stems festooned with moss and their trunks surrounded by emerging ferns. The dramatic form and striking colour of these four magnificent specimens of Acer palmatum, which stand beside the path that leads down from the High Walk (Chapter 6), provide a dramatic finale to the Maple Walk

Opposite: Brantwood, from the eastern shore of Coniston Water – now, as in Ruskin's day, an important point of arrival and departure for visitors to the house. The ancient coppiced woodland (Chapter 2) in which Brantwood's gardens are set clothes the hillside behind the house, while the wildflower meadow (Chapter 7) may be seen stretching out to the left between the house and the lakeside

FOREWORD

When David Ingram approached me to say that he would like to write a short introduction to Brantwood's gardens, I was delighted. He suggested, at first, a brief guide of maybe eight pages. 'Of course,' said David in an unguarded moment, 'there really is a book here.' From then on there was no looking back. That such a distinguished figure in the field of botanical science should bend his gaze upon Ruskin and Brantwood had long been my hope but scarcely dared to be my expectation. Ruskin would have appreciated the manner in which the ensuing project grew from modest ambition into the handsome and important study that awaits the reader. It may not quite have expanded into the five volumes of Ruskin's *Modern Painters* that grew out of a magazine article on Turner, but I imagine that there have been days when David felt as if it might!

It comes as something of a surprise to most people to consider Ruskin the Gardener. Ruskin has been much written about as an art critic and is admired for his beautiful watercolours; he is famous as a powerful voice on social and economic justice, and even championed as a prophet of climate change. Yet all Ruskin's writings grow from the fertile soil of specific places. Brantwood is one of three special places – Chamonix and Venice are the others – that sit at the heart of his work.

As David Ingram makes clear, however, the seeds sown by Ruskin at Brantwood have, by a remarkable process of conjugation and confrontation, produced some extraordinary offspring. This is really a book about three gardens, or – more precisely – three gardeners, Ruskin, Severn and Beamish. I came to Brantwood in 1996 at a time when Sally Beamish was already under way with her inspired contribution to this story. She had started important restorations and begun new additions which spoke to the past but were looking forward as well. It has been a joy and a privilege over the years to work with her and her team of gardeners and volunteers as they have revealed so much of the past and added so much more to the present.

Visitors to Brantwood often remark upon the special atmosphere of the place, so it is fair to ask 'What makes it so special?' Brantwood is not of great age; people have not worshipped here over millennia; there are no ancient circles or burial mounds. The many signs of woodland industry suggest it was a work-a-day sort of place: that is all. The view from Brantwood is spectacular, but the Lakes are full of wonderful views – and

Opposite: English bluebells, their delicate azure blue flowers and heavenly scent evoking a sense of timelessness, carpet the woodland floor in late spring. The bluebells of Brantwood, like the gardens, are gently evolving, however: originally they will all have all been the native Hyacinthoides non-scriptus, *with its characteristic nodding, one sided spikes of flowers, but now some flowers show evidence of hybridization with the more robust Spanish bluebell* (H. hispanica), *of garden origin, which has flatter, paler blue flowers arranged all round an upright spike*

even the view from the London Eye isn't bad. The answer lies in the ethos that Ruskin planted at Brantwood. It is no accident that culture and cultivation derive from the same root. The particular marriage of wild nature and human husbandry that Ruskin affirmed, when approached in the right spirit, can produce something altogether magical and life enhancing – an environment of physical and spiritual sustenance. Professor Ingram's book traces the evolution of this once unpromising patch of land, through vision, affection and hard work, into a place of great inspiration.

I consider this book to be one of the loveliest gifts the gardeners – and the gardens - could have been given in reward for their years of toil on our steep, rainy and rocky slopes. I am deeply indebted to David for undertaking it.

Howard Hull

Brantwood, March 2014

Opposite: Estate-produced fence posts and rails, products of the present-day coppiced woodland of Brantwood (Chapter 2), are little different now from how they might have looked in Ruskin's time. They have a simple, elegant beauty and soon weather, providing a habitat for algae, lichens and moss as they become part of the living landscape from which they sprang as saplings

PREFACE

This short book about the gardens of Brantwood, John Ruskin's home in the English Lake District from 1872 until his death in 1900, was compiled for three reasons. Firstly, because I fell in love at first sight with this idiosyncratic group of gardens and their woodland setting, and wanted to share my pleasure with others by providing an accessible introduction to them. Secondly, because I wished to set down for future generations a snapshot in time of the gardens as I saw them throughout 2012 and 2013. And finally, because writing about the gardens gave me a legitimate excuse for the self-indulgence of visiting them once or twice a month for almost two years.

Much has changed at Brantwood since 1903, when the last such account of the gardens was published by W. G. Collingwood in *Ruskin's Relics*. The gardens of John Ruskin and his cousin Joan Severn, whose remarkable creations were only referred to in passing by Collingwood, were, like an enchanted paradise in a fairy tale, gradually engulfed by the luxuriant growth of wild nature for most of the ensuing century, eventually to be miraculously restored to life by the commitment, skill and boundless creative energy of a new Head Gardener, Sally Beamish, from 1988 onwards. Moreover, Sally opened up and began to manage the woodland surrounding the gardens and also added exciting new gardens of her own design, based on what she describes as 'Ruskinian principles', that perfectly complement the gardens of Ruskin and Severn. The result is an utterly delightful garden landscape set on the eastern shore of one of the most beautiful of the English lakes.

In the interests of brevity the book is essentially descriptive. Analysis of what the gardens can tell us about Ruskin as artist and art critic, plant scientist, naturalist, gardener and social reformer, about the inspiration behind Joan Severn's gardens and her standing as a garden designer, or about Sally Beamish's vision for a 'Ruskinian' approach to gardening in the twenty-first century, except for relatively short comments among the descriptions, will have to wait for a more detailed academic treatment. For me, however, in the words of the late Seamus Heaney, quoting Gerard Manley Hopkins, the nineteenth century poet whom Ruskin admired: 'Description is revelation…' Much has certainly been revealed to me while writing the descriptions embodied in this book, and my mind is now full of ideas for future projects. I do hope that all who are led to and guided around the gardens of Brantwood by this account will be similarly stimulated.

Opposite: Blossom of an espalier-trained pear tree growing against the wall at the top of Zig-zaggy

The book came about because, having been working on an exhibition of Ruskin's botanical drawings in the Ruskin Library of Lancaster University, I felt that I might be better able to understand many of them if I were to re-visit the gardens of their creator. Accordingly Howard Hull, Director of Brantwood, together with Sally Beamish, gave me a wonderful and enlightening tour early in 2012. When the time came for me to leave, however, and I asked if I might purchase a booklet about the gardens, I was disappointed to be told that only a brief leaflet-map existed. On my return home I resolved to write a short guide myself. I sketched an outline of what I had in mind and sent it off to Howard and Sally for their comments. They were both enthusiastic about the project and urged me to start work as soon as possible. I began gathering information in early summer 2012 and commenced writing in January 2013, thinking that my guide might be in print by Easter. How wrong I was: I soon realised that I had so much material that it would not be possible to do the gardens justice in a short guide and that a complete book was required. I put the suggestion to Howard who, instead of rejecting my proposal out of hand as I expected, called my bluff by saying that he had hoped all along that this might be the outcome.

Although the resulting book is based on my own observations and research, its production has been very much a team effort, and it could not have been created without the help and hard work of several key people. First and foremost, Sally Beamish has been generous to a fault with her time, ideas, recollections, written material and constructive comments on the draft text. Wherever I have enriched the book by quoting her verbatim, as I have also done with the words of Ruskin, Collingwood and Hull, this has been clearly acknowledged. There are, however, other instances scattered throughout the text where I have paraphrased or summarised Sally's spoken or written words without acknowledgement, and I am deeply grateful to her for allowing me to do so.

Howard Hull has been a constant source of encouragement, advice and information throughout the project. The results of his unobtrusive but inspired management style are everywhere evident at Brantwood, and during the writing of the book he has been a fount of wisdom whose gentle steers have on many occasions set my wandering mind on the right path. He has, moreover, been a most constructive critic of draft text material and has provided an invaluable service at a critical time, ably assisted by Ron Ward, a Brantwood volunteer, in assembling illustrations.

Ruth and Dave Charles, gardeners at Brantwood, have been extremely generous in providing, often at short notice, photographs and written material for me to adapt, especially for the lists of plants, and in reading and providing thoughtful and constructive comments on the draft text, and I thank them both most warmly for their support and dedication. Stephen Wildman, Rebecca Patterson, Diane Tyler and Jen Shepherd of the Ruskin Library in Lancaster University have been invaluable and highly knowledgeable sources of information, documents and archive photographs relating to the gardens and I thank them for their never-failing patience and professionalism. I further acknowledge the great debt I owe to the authors of the written sources I drew on for historical and background material: Ruskin and Collingwood, of course, but also especially James Dearden and Fiona Loynes. Likewise I am most grateful to those who have generously provided the photographs and other illustrations that illuminate the text, all of whom are individually acknowledged elsewhere.

Alison Ingram has given her generous and unfailing help and support throughout the making of the book. Her contribution to this, as to many other projects, has been immense.

Alexander Fyjis-Walker's professional editorial and design skills are evident throughout the printed version of the book and I thank him for doing such a splendid job.

And finally I wish to thank all the staff of Brantwood for enabling me to share and enjoy the unique Lakeland paradise they care for and clearly love. Inspired by what must be one of the most beautiful working environments imaginable, their unfailing courtesy, kindness and generosity of spirit has known no bounds.

David Ingram
North Berwick, East Lothian, Scotland
March 2014

BRANTWOOD HORTICULTURAL AND WOODLAND WORKFORCE SINCE c. 1980

Any attempt to give credit for a project which has been sustained over such a long time inevitably falls far short of being comprehensive. The following lists the principal people involved, some of whom were employed for many years and made a major contribution, and some of whom, such as students and recently qualified gardeners, worked for short periods, gaining a unique experience whilst at the same time giving valuable assistance. Of continuing and invaluable significance have been the many volunteers, too numerous to list, who have contributed selflessly over many years.

Early 1980s–1990s   Bruce Hanson (joint Manager) organised Youth Training Scheme and Manpower Services Commission teams to begin work on making Brantwood's environs safe for a growing number of visitors. This included provision for car parking, walling, work on the jetty approach, the laying of hard surfaces around the buildings, tree felling and scrub clearance. A general appeal was made locally for plant donations.

1987   Sally Beamish joined Brantwood, as a volunteer, to help plan more detailed horticulture work and to develop initial planting plans for the areas around the house and leading to the lake shore.

1988   Sally Beamish made Head Gardener and began the task of garden restoration. Two assistants normally support Sally Beamish in her work – initially mid-course students from Askham Bryan College and Myerscough College.

Early 1990s onwards   Permanent garden staff appointed, with occasional student interns and an active programme of local volunteers. The workforce included, at various times: Bill Atkinson (farmer and forester), Ray Bragg (who assisted Sally Beamish for ten years with many of the intensely physical challenges associated with the early stages of garden restoration), Bernie Brunt, Chris Corbridge, Brian Crosland (dry-stone waller), Gundula Deutschlander (who played a key role in the Zig-zaggy restoration), Maureen Fleming (longest-standing of many volunteers), Masako Fukuwatari, Lynn Hardie, Rosamund Henley, Mark Kynham, Liz Leahey, Anne Lowes, Barbara Morze-Diethelm, Ros Newberry, Chris Nuttall, Elly Sinclair, Alex Smith, Malcolm Smith, David Spenceley, James Taylor and Sylvia Villega.

Help also came from The Conservation Volunteers (formerly BTCV); and many other organisations and individuals.

Opposite: The Brantwood garden staff on a summer day in 2009: from left to right, Ruth Charles (Gardener), Sally Beamish (Head Gardener), Dave Charles (Gardener) and Peter Wright (Master of Practical Trades)

1. OVERVIEW

The unique Lakeland landscape garden at Brantwood, set on a hillside facing west across Coniston Water, comprises a series of exquisite jewel-like garden islands (hereafter referred to as gardens) set in a wider sea of ancient woodland of sessile oak, hazel and other species. (See sketch map on p. 119.) The woodland was once coppiced for industry and commerce, but is now carefully managed to perfectly complement the gardens and to provide an important haven for wild flowers, insects, birds and other animals. All the gardens are interconnected by a labyrinth of paths and walks through the woodland, while the ever changing and ravishingly beautiful borrowed landscape of Coniston Water and the surrounding fells is constantly revealed by strategically placed openings and vistas. The first group of new gardens was created, and the woodlands managed as a setting for them, by John Ruskin – one of the towering intellectual giants of the nineteenth century – immediately following his purchase of Brantwood in 1871 and his permanent move there in 1872.

Further gardens were laid out towards the end of the nineteenth century by Joan Severn (*née* Agnew), another talented garden maker. She was Ruskin's cousin, and after caring for his mother in her later years, eventually became his châtelaine at Brantwood – the 'lady of the house' – for housekeeper is far too mundane a title for someone so important in the Ruskin establishment. Joan Severn was also destined to play another significant role in Ruskin's life, as his carer during his long, final illness, when his creative genius was quenched and his gardens left untended and overwhelmed by weeds. After Ruskin's death in 1900 Joan Severn's gardens continued to flourish for a time, but following her own death in 1924, nature gradually engulfed all until 1936, when the Friends of Brantwood made significant early attempts to restore the gardens. It was not until the 1980s, however, following three key appointments, that the present-day structure of the estate and gardens began to emerge. First Bruce Hanson was appointed Joint Manager of the Brantwood House and Estate (1982-95); then, in 1988, a young horticulturist of vision, Sally Beamish, was made Head Gardener; and finally, in 1996, Howard Hull was appointed Director, and has since played an invaluable role as the inspirational leader of the whole Brantwood enterprise, of which the woodland and gardens are integral parts.

Gradually Sally Beamish, with the assistance of her students, staff (see p. 15) and a complement of dedicated volunteers, began to re-manage the woodland, release the gardens of Ruskin and Joan Severn from their long slumber and, with great sensitivity and skill,

Opposite: A serious, elegantly clad and groomed John Ruskin, wide-brimmed hat beside him, sitting by a dry-stone wall at Brantwood in 1873, the year in which work on Zig-zaggy began (Chapter 4)

restore and in some cases completely renovate them. Moreover, she began to add to this unique landscape entirely new gardens of her own design, based on what she describes as 'Ruskinian principles'.

The whole landscape, although apparently static to the visitor's eye, is now, as in Ruskin's day, in a state of gentle evolutionary change. The management of the woodland and the plantings in the gardens are adjusted year on year, as disease and harsh weather take their toll. Things may also change as different associations and arrangements suggest themselves to the horticultural staff and as they come to better understand the micro-climate and soil of a particular site, or as aesthetic, investigative or educational priorities change. Moreover, from time to time and for similar reasons, some garden areas may be totally re-planted, or unfinished designs completed or, indeed, entirely new gardens created.

Thus Brantwood embodies the hard work and vision of three creative minds, each serving a different audience: John Ruskin, whose management of the woodland and creation of the first gardens combined the exploration of new ideas and concepts with aesthetically pleasing plantings primarily for his own eyes and thoughts; Joan Severn, whose gardens were decorative and created for her own pleasure and for that of a small circle of family and friends; and Sally Beamish, who has made the woodland, the Ruskin and Severn gardens and her own Ruskin-inspired gardens accessible to thousands of visitors every year. Although interconnected, the woodland and the gardens each have their own distinctive characters, which will be explored in the following pages, enriched by the words of their creators and those of W. G. Collingwood, Ruskin's pupil, secretary and first biographer, and by contemporary drawings, paintings and photographs. First, however, it is important to consider the estate as a whole, including the wider landscape and woodland that provide an indispensable and complementary setting for the gardens.

Opposite: Brantwood from the edge of Coniston Water, by John Ruskin. This simple pencil, watercolour and bodycolour sketch on paper was made during Ruskin's first visit to the house on 12th September 1871 and sent to his cousin Joan Severn to show her what his new acquisition looked like. The later inscription by Joan reads: 'Brantwood by JR, before additions'

Brantwood by JR[?]
before additions.

2. THE SETTING

THE ESTATE

During the summer of 1871, when Ruskin was recovering from serious illness at Matlock, in Derbyshire, he heard that Brantwood had been put up for sale by William James Linton, artist, poet, political writer, botanist and wood engraver of distinction. Ruskin, who had known Coniston since childhood, although not the house itself, immediately offered Linton the asking price of £1500, sight unseen. This was accepted and in September he visited his new property for the first time. Included in the sale were sixteen acres (c. 6.5 hectares) of land, which, like the house, commanded what Ruskin described in a letter to his friend C. E. Norton as:

> five acres of rock and moor, a streamlet, and I think on the whole the finest view
> I know in Cumberland or Lancashire.

In a letter to another correspondent, the Scottish philosopher and historian Thomas Carlyle, he said that it was:

> a bit of steep hillside, facing west… The slope is half copse, half moor and rock – a
> pretty field beneath, less steep – a white two storied cottage, and a bank of turf in
> front of it – then a narrow mountain road and on the other side of that – Naboth's
> Vineyard – my neighbour's field, to the water's edge...

In his *Memories* (1894), Linton says that during his occupation of Brantwood he rented a garden and two fields between the house and the lake, and had another small garden behind the house with bees, reached by steps to above the height of the house. Linton also kept livestock, including some twenty sheep that grazed the fells above Brantwood. When the fells were enclosed, this small flock entitled him to a parcel of six acres (c. 2.4 hectares) of the common fell land, which increased the size of the estate to the sixteen acres purchased by Ruskin in 1871. Ruskin added to the estate at various times after 1871 by renting adjacent land and later by purchasing one small piece of ground. Then in 1885, in view of his deteriorating health, he made over the house and garden to the family of Joan Severn and her husband, the artist Arthur Severn, although it remained nominally his own until his death. During the following ten years Mrs Severn made several more purchases of land, thereby increasing the size of the estate to some 500 acres

William James Linton, who lived at Brantwood from 1852 until 1871. Linton, who described himself as a 'radical artisan', edited the political magazine The English Republic, *which he printed in an outbuilding on the south drive. One of his slogans, 'God and the People', is still visible in the upstairs room that once housed the press and which today provides a home for an updated version of Ruskin's musical 'lithophone', constructed from the different rocks of Cumbria*

Opposite: A view from the path above the Maple Walk, looking over the spectacular red canopy of the four (until recently five) venerable Japanese Acer palmatum *trees towards the western shore of Coniston Water and the Coniston fells rising up from it*

Crag Head in winter. This wind-swept spot is above the Moorland Garden and is the highest point on the Brantwood Estate.

(c. 202 hectares), double what it is today. The new land included: Thurston, at that time known as Coniston Bank; Low Bank Ground; Lawson Park Farm, a medieval sheep park established on the adjacent fells by the monks of Furness Abbey; and in the lake, Fir Island, now owned by the National Trust. The property stretched for almost a mile and a quarter (c. 2 km) along the road on the eastern side of the lake, from near Lanehead to Beck Leven, although the total length higher up the hillside was closer to a mile and a half (c. 2.4 km).

Joan Severn died in 1924, and following the subsequent death of Arthur Severn in 1931 the house and estate were sold by auction. Eight lots, comprising the house, outbuildings and 250 acres (c. 101 hectares) of land were acquired 'for the nation' for £7000, by John Howard Whitehouse, founder and headmaster of Bembridge School on the Isle of Wight, and Ruskin scholar, disciple and collector, who had been endeavouring to purchase the estate for a number of years. Following an unsuccessful attempt to gift the house and estate in perpetuity to Oxford University, Whitehouse passed them to his own foundation, Education Trust Ltd, in whose care they remain.

Opposite: A magnificent specimen of the rhododendron 'May Day' in full flower beside the estate-made rustic gate leading out of the lower end of the Professor's Garden (Chapter 4)

The land acquired by Whitehouse included, in the 250 acres, half a mile (c. 0.8 km) of lake shore, from which the ground rises steeply first through pasture, then through some 100 acres (c. 40.5 hectares) of mixed sessile oak/hazel woodland to regenerating woodland, and finally to the fell tops. The estate now includes a diversity of habitats and ecosystems rich in wild flowers and wildlife, including, in addition to the woodland itself, marsh, hay-meadows, upland pasture and heathy moor tops. These habitats and their biodiversity are all carefully managed and conserved by Brantwood's staff, and the gardens must, therefore, be seen as an integral part of this ecological mix.

THE WOODLAND

Before describing the gardens in detail, it is important to take a close look at the species-rich woodland in which they are set.

Beginnings

Brant is an old Norse word meaning 'steep', in this case referring to a wood standing on the eastern shore of the lake originally called Thurston Mere, a name also from old Norse that persisted well into the eighteenth century, when an alternative name, Coniston Water, supplanted it. The long, narrow lake, which is up to *c*. 184 feet (*c*. 56 metres) deep in places, runs roughly north-south and lies in a deep, U-shaped valley gouged out of the volcanic, metamorphic and other rocks by a glacier during the Devensian Glaciation (often referred to as the 'last Ice age', which lasted from about 110,000 years to 11,600 years before the present). Brantwood thus has an approximately north-western aspect, facing across the lake towards Coniston village, the Old Man of Coniston (*c*. 2635 feet; *c*. 803 metres.) and the adjacent fells. The soil is largely acidic, with base-rich (lime-laden) 'flushes', some of which are boggy.

Until the twelfth century the lower slopes of the Coniston fells were covered with thick, ancient wildwood, leaving only the higher ground free of trees to sustain the grazing of the relatively small numbers of animals kept by the subsistence farmers who inhabited the area. During the reign of Henry II (1154-89), however, the lands to the east of the lake were acquired by the monks of Furness Abbey, a wealthy Cistercian foundation established in 1123.

Sheep farming and woodland industries

The monks required more from the land than simply the support of subsistence agriculture, and began to exploit it for a diversity of other purposes. The principal one of these was wool production by tenant sheep farmers who grazed their animals on the high ground in the summer months but brought them down to the lower, wooded slopes during the winter. There the trees provided shelter and the undergrowth and evergreen shrubby species, such as holly, supplementary rough grazing ('pannage'), for which the tenant farmers paid a 'grenehewe' rent to the Abbey. This practice would inevitably have had an adverse effect on the growth and regeneration of the woodland vegetation.

Opposite: Dryad's Saddle or scaly bracket fungus (Polyporus squamosus) growing from the moss covered trunk of a decaying tree. This parasitic fungus, which produces its spores in pores, instead of gills, on the underside of the cap, is the cause of an intensive white rot in many tree species, especially sycamore, beech and elm. Wood rotting fungi are an ever-present threat to wounded or weakened trees in ancient woodland. Such deaths are not an end, however, for they open gaps in the canopy, allowing sun-loving plants to flower for a time and new tree seedlings to become established

Herdwick sheep, a hardy breed native to, and almost confined to, the Lake District. Perhaps introduced by Norse settlers, Herdwicks are low in lambing capacity and produce coarse wool. They are prized, however, for their robust health, their ability to live solely on forage and their territorial instincts, which prevent them straying too far over the rough Lakeland fells. The survival of Herdwicks was threatened by the 2001 outbreak of foot and mouth disease, but intense local effort has resulted in the breed remaining a central part of traditional Lakeland agriculture

The ancient skill of charcoal burning is still maintained at Brantwood, as here. Instead of being used for iron smelting as in the past, however, the charcoal is now used as fuel for barbecues, for slug control and 'sweetening' garden soil and composts, and for use by artists

Moreover, as time went by and the demand for wool increased, some areas of the woodland on the lower slopes were probably clear-felled to yield yet more land for summer grazing. Such use of grazed 'intakes' in the woodland area is a practice still in use today, and is reflected in the name Long Intake on Brantwood's northern boundary.

At the same time, the woods began to be managed in order to sustain a variety of woodland industries. A report of the revenues of the Abbey, made in 1537 by Commissioners appointed by Henry VIII prior to the Dissolution of the Monasteries, lists several of these, although possibly not all. Most importantly, various native tree species would have been cut for making charcoal, which was used for smelting iron and subsequently copper. Very much later, the finest charcoal, for the manufacture of gunpowder, would have been made from the alder that grew in the wetter parts of the wood, a practice commemorated in the name 'Gunpowder Wood' on land adjacent to Brantwood.

Another important industry from the earliest times was the harvesting of oak bark, rich in the polyphenol tannin, which was required for tanning hides to produce leather (the production of oak bark for tanning continues in the woods of the Furness Peninsula to the present day). Oak timber would also have been used by coopers for making barrel staves, while larger timbers would have been employed in constructing houses and other buildings. Coarse matting and swill baskets were probably woven from thin lathes of young oak and hazel, and hazel stems may have been turned for making simple furniture. The bark fibres (bast) of small-leaved lime could have been twisted to make rope. And straight-grained and flexible ash wood, which grew near the base-rich flushes, for ash is a lime-loving tree, was used by wheelwrights and others for making cartwheels, the saddle-trees for pack animals and the handles and hafts of agricultural tools. Various woods, but especially water-resistant elm wood, may have been turned for making cups and bowls, while alder, still found growing in the wetter parts of the wood and beside the becks, could have been used for making the soles of clogs.

Coppicing

Such intensive use of the woodland would have required careful management and it is likely that the practice of 'coppicing' would have been introduced fairly early on. This ancient form of management depends on the regrowth of trees following felling. First, the areas of the woodland to be coppiced are enclosed, often with dry-stone walls in Lakeland, to protect new growth from browsing animals. Then widely spaced maiden

A woodland sculpture by Malcolm Smith, surrounded by regenerating hazel coppice stools

Hazel stool, new cut, at the start of the coppice cycle

Wood anemone (Anemone nemerosa) –
'Silvia', as Ruskin called it – flowering profusely in the spring sunlight let through to the woodland floor by coppicing. The characteristic variegated, arrowhead shaped leaves of Arum italicum subsp. italicum *'Marmoratum' (or* A. italicum *'Pictum' as it is often known), may be seen amongst the flowers*

Opposite: Hazel poles regenerating from mature coppice stools close to the estate wall

(uncut) trees are selected for retention, so that they may grow on to full maturity. These are the 'standards' of a 'coppice with standards' system, and some may still be found at Brantwood as fine old 'character veterans'. Next, selected young trees are cut down close to the ground, to create 'coppice stools' – the bases of the trees set on their original rootstocks – that regenerate to produce long, straight sticks or larger poles, as required for various woodland industries. Older trees, which are generally less likely to re-grow, are removed. Many tree seedlings become established in the open, light conditions and disturbed soils resulting from the felling, however, and some of these may be retained to fill in the gaps created in the coppice structure by the removal of the old trees.

Coppicing would have been repeated at Brantwood on a regular rotation of about eight to thirty years, depending on tree species and the end products required, perhaps for centuries. Indeed, W. G. Collingwood believed that some of the very largest coppice stools on the estate in the late nineteenth century probably dated back to the Middle Ages, while recent research suggests that some of the massive small-leaved lime stools still to be seen at Brantwood have survived for more than 2,500 years.

An aesthetic bonus of coppicing, used to advantage in the woodland today, is that the felling at the start of the cycle lets in the daylight, resulting in the abundant blooming for a few years of plants such as bluebells, primroses, wild garlic (ramsons) and wood anemones, all previously kept in check by the deep shade cast by the tree canopy. Gradually the regenerating trees re-establish the shade, thereby suppressing the flowering plants once more, until the next round of coppicing commences and the 'bloom and bust' cycle begins again.

Iron and copper smelting

The management of the woodlands by coppicing on the eastern shore of Coniston Water (then Thurston Mere) was originally closely associated with metal smelting. Copper had been mined and smelted in the area since Roman times, but it was the smelting of iron in the Middle Ages that would have placed the greatest demand for charcoal on the adjacent woodland. The sites of iron 'bloomeries', primitive structures for smelting iron ore that preceded the coke-fired blast-furnaces of the industrial revolution, have been found both on and around the Brantwood estate.

The monks of Furness had worked iron ore in Low Furness since the middle of the thirteenth century, with the result that much of their timber was soon exhausted. Rather

Discarded clinker-fused iron, charcoal and rock from an old iron smelting site ('bloomery') near Brantwood

than import bulky timber from elsewhere (it takes about five tons [I ton = 1,016 kilograms] of wood to produce a ton of charcoal for the smelting/purifying process), it made sense to take the more compact iron ore to the wooded lake-shore around Thurston Mere for smelting there, especially as water was itself required for this process. Collingwood has suggested that there is a close correlation in this area between the sites of Furness Abbey 'parks', areas of woodland cleared to create new grazing land, and the sites of the Abbey bloomeries. For example, Beck Leven bloomery, in the south-western corner of the present Brantwood estate, is situated immediately below Lawson (formerly Lowson) Park, a Furness Abbey sheep farm. Thus it would seem that the monks found it expedient to integrate these two aspects of woodland exploitation, probably moving bloomeries closer to the next area scheduled for clearance, once the land about an existing site had become devoid of trees.

By the middle of the sixteenth century the demands of the bloomeries for charcoal were so great that other woodland industries suffered. Accordingly, iron smelting was suppressed in 1565, but as is the way of things, was soon replaced by copper smelting, especially following the opening of the Coniston copper mines by German immigrants towards the end of the century. Some of the charcoal-burning sites found at Brantwood today may date from this period, although others may be newer, since commercial charcoal burning continued in the area until the early twentieth century.

Dissolution of the Monasteries

In 1537 Furness Abbey, like the other monasteries in England, was dissolved on the orders of Henry VIII and its lands passed to the Crown. A period of uncertainty followed and tenancies were not stabilised until the end of the sixteenth century. Eventually, in 1662, the Abbey lands were transferred by Charles II to private landlords, although the tenancies were largely unaffected by this change. By the time John Ruskin purchased Brantwood in 1871, none of the original wildwood would have remained. Instead, there would have been common grazing land on the high fells and, lower down the slope, richer grazing land created by woodland clearance, degraded woodland resulting from over-exploitation, and enclosed woodland still managed by coppicing.

It has already been emphasised that the woodland should not be regarded merely as a backdrop for the gardens, but rather as a dynamic and integral part of the Brantwood garden landscape. The horticultural team devotes considerable thought and energy to the presentation of the woodland, which is thus given as much attention as any of the garden islands. The principal native trees in the wood today are listed on p. 34 as are the principal shrubby, understorey species.

A number of green-leaved, exotic tree and shrubby species act as a foil for the native trees and provide a background for other flowering or brightly coloured exotics (also listed on p. 34). In addition, a collection of birches (*Betula* spp.) is being developed in the Fern Garden (see p. 93) and two rare Chinese limes (*Tillia callidonta* and *T. chinensis*) are to be found in a field at the edge of the estate.

*The unfurling fronds of the native hart's tongue fern (*Asplenium scolopendrium*) in the woodland at Brantwood*

Light is relatively scarce beneath the trees, especially in summer, but many herbaceous species nevertheless thrive in the cool, damp semi-shade, especially close to the paths and in the more open areas. At Brantwood these include: the green-flowered dog's mercury (*Mercurialis perennis*) and wood sage (*Teucrium scorodonia*); herb bennett or wood avens (*Geum urbanum*); delicate wood sorrel (*Oxalis acetosella*) and violets – especially sweet violet (*Viola odorata*) and common dog violet (*V. riviana*); primroses (*Primula vulgaris*) and false oxlips (*P.* x *polyantha*, a hybrid of primrose and cowslip); bulbous species such as pale gold, wild daffodil hybrids (*Narcissus pseudonarcissus* hybrids), native bluebells (*Hyacinthoides non-scriptus*) and hybrids of this species and the garden bluebell (*H. hispanica*), and the strongly smelling wild garlic (ramsons; *Allium ursinum*); and the green-stemmed, shrubby bilberry (*Vaccinium myrtillus*) and exotic *Vaccinium* species. Also present are shade-tolerant grasses, woodrushes (*Luzula campestris* and other *Luzula* spp.), native ferns, including the robust, shuttlecock-shaped scaly male fern (*Dryopteris affinis*), the more dainty lady fern (*Athyrium filix-femina*), both of which die back in winter, and the winter-green common polypody (*Polypodium vulgare*) and hart's tongue (*Asplenium scolopendrium*). Finally, the ground is carpeted with a great diversity of mosses and leafy liverworts (a detailed survey of the mosses and liverworts at Brantwood is urgently required).

Although the practice of coppicing was abandoned by Ruskin for aesthetic reasons, as will be discussed later, it was recently re-established, for woodland cannot be left for any considerable period of time without management or it becomes overgrown and

impenetrable. The coppicing now serves to keep parts of the woodland visually accessible, creating ever-changing vistas within and beyond the trees and encouraging a diversity of habitats and species. For example, coppicing creates open sites where the seed of long-dormant species such as foxgloves may be stimulated to grow and flower by exposure to the light. Moreover, other perennial native woodland plants such as those listed above benefit greatly from the extra light. In some areas colourful, interesting or unusual species and cultivars of small shade-tolerant trees and shrubs have been planted, alone or in small groups, to provide highlights and points of special interest such as blossom in spring and summer, or fruits and intense leaf colour in autumn (p. 34).

Coppicing and other management practices, such as the provision of log-piles and brash, leaving some areas undisturbed, fencing other areas to prevent public access, providing badger gates and controlling grey squirrels, all help to encourage wildlife by creating habitats, nesting and roosting sites and food sources to enable a wide diversity of species to thrive and breed (see p. 35).

Moreover, the living trees support the growth on their roots of beneficial, symbiotic fungi (mycorrhiza) and often, on roots, leaves or stems, parasitic fungi that cause disease. The dead wood left behind by coppicing makes a perfect substrate for the growth of saprophytic fungi that break down dead organic matter and return it to the soil. Many of these fellow travellers produce spore-bearing fruiting bodies such as toadstools or cups, often brightly coloured, especially during the cool, damp weeks of autumn.

Last, but by no means least, coppicing, with its cycles of felling and regeneration, helps to maintain the ancient semi-natural status of Brantwood's woodland. By re-introducing coppice systems, the staff of Brantwood may now practise and teach coppicing and many other greenwood skills, thereby helping to conserve such traditional Lakeland crafts. Home-produced fence posts and rails, hazel hurdles, riven-wood (for steps), hazel and birch plant-supports, wind-breaks and wood sculptures are all used on the estate, as they probably were in Ruskin's time. Such products have a simple beauty and soon weather to become part of the landscape, rather than opposing it as commercially produced wooden landscaping materials might do. Moreover, different grades of charcoal, for barbecues, slug control, 'sweetening' soil and composts, and for use by artists, are all produced at Brantwood – the adaptation of an old process to make products of value in the modern world. The application of many traditional skills, together with recycling, make the estate, woodland and gardens extremely self-sufficient as regards materials, the staff making the best use of everything available.

Opposite: A tranquil late spring morning in the woodland, with Ruskin's Pond just visible among the trees and bluebells

WOODLAND FLORA

The principal native large and small trees occurring in the woodland areas

Deciduous
sessile oak *Quercus petraea*
hazel *Corylus avellana*
    together with:
alder *Alnus glutinosa* – in the
    wetter places
ash *Fraxinus excelsior* – near
    lime-laden flushes
beech *Fagus sylvatica* – a small
    number
goat willow *Salix caprea*
hornbeam *Carpinus betulus* –
    a small number
rowan *Sorbus aucuparia*
silver and downy birches *Betula*
    pendula and *B. pubescens*
small-leaved lime *Tilia cordata*
sycamore *Acer pseudoplatanus*
wild cherry [gean] *Prunus avium*

Evergreen
Scots pine *Pinus sylvestris* –
    a few on the higher ground
yew *Taxus baccata*

The principal shrubby native species forming the understorey of the woodland

Deciduous
blackthorn *Prunus spinosa*
bramble *Rubus fruticosa*
gorse *Ulex europaeus*
guelder rose *Viburnum opulus* –
    occasionally
hawthorn *Crataegus monogyna*
honeysuckle *Lonicera periclymenum*
wild rose *Rosa canina*

Evergreen
holly *Ilex aquifolium*
juniper *Juniperus communis* –
    especially on higher ground

The principal green-leaved exotic trees and shrubby species in the woodland

Broadleaf, deciduous
maples *Acer* spp.

Coniferous, deciduous
European larch *Larix europaea*
maidenhair tree *Ginkgo biloba*

Coniferous, evergreen
Brewer's weeping spruce *Picea*
    breweriana
deodar cedar *Cedrus deodara*
Japanese red cedar *Cryptomeria*
    japonica
Lawson cypress *Chamaecyparis*
    lawsoniana
Norway spruce *Picea abies*
western hemlock *Tsuga hetero-*
    phylla

Colourful (leaves, flowers, fruit or autumn leaf colour), small shade-tolerant tree and shrub species and cultivars planted in the woodland for aesthetic effect

barberries *Berberis*
dogwoods *Cornus*
elders *Sambucus*
hawthorns *Crataegus*
hydrangeas *Hydrangea*
ironwoods *Parrotia*
Japanese and other maples *Acer*
katsuras *Cercidiphyllum*
magnolias *Magnolia*
rowans (mountain ash) and rela-
    tives *Sorbus*
pieris *Pieris*
rhododendrons *Rhododendron*
serviceberries *Amelanchier*
sumachs *Rhus*
tree peonies *Paeonia*
viburnums *Viburnum*

WOODLAND FAUNA

Brantwood's woodland provides excellent habitats for wildlife. For example, over 60 different varieties of birds have been identified. Some of the birds, mammals and other animals that may be observed in the woodland are listed below:

Birds

barn owl
black grouse
black-headed gull
blackbird
blue tit
bullfinch
buzzard
Canada goose
carrion crow
chaffinch
coal tit
coot
common gull
cormorant
cuckoo
dipper
goldcrest
great crested grebe
great spotted woodpecker
great tit
green woodpecker
greenfinch
grey wagtail
heron
hedge sparrow
herring gull
house martin
house sparrow
jackdaw
jay
kestrel
lesser black-backed gull

linnet
little grebe
long-tailed tit
magpie
mallard
marsh tit
meadow pipit
mistle thrush
mute swan
pheasant
pied wagtail
raven
red kite
redpoll
redstart
robin
rook
song thrush
starling
swallow
tawny owl
treecreeper
tufted duck
whinchat
woodpigeon
wren
yellow wagtail

Mammals

badger
bats (pipistrelle, long-eared)
deer (red, roe)
fox

grey squirrel
hedgehog
mice
polecat
rabbit
red squirrel
shrew
stoat
vole
weasel

Reptiles

adder
grass snake
lizard
slow-worm

Amphibians

common newt (and perhaps
    crested – someone who
    ought to know said they
    once almost sat on one)
frog
toad

Smaller Creatures

Snails, slugs, spiders etc. The insect life is too numerous to detail, including as it does a large variety of beetles, bees (bumble- and honey-), butterflies, dragonflies, hoverflies, moths (notably the rare netted carpet moth) and wasps.

Studies of larch buds by John Ruskin. These two drawings, one in pen and ink and the other in pencil, watercolour and bodycolour, are of the young female buds (developing cones) of the deciduous European larch (Larix decidua; syn. L. europea), an introduced tree species planted at Brantwood and elsewhere in the Lake District. It is not known whether the studies were actually made at Brantwood, but in a letter of 1875 Ruskin does refer to a 'long spray of larch with purple buds' (usually described as being reddish rather than purple).

These studies are testimony to Ruskin's passionate observation of even the smallest aspects of the natural world (these buds may well have been about a centimetre long) and to the astonishing ease with which he handles very different media for different purposes. In the line drawing, right, reproduced here slightly larger than actual size, Ruskin examines the architecture of the cone and its fixing to the twig; in the watercolour opposite, reproduced slightly smaller than actual size, he gives full expression to the brilliant hues of the bud, whose intensity he conveys by colouring the entire background.

Writing of another conifer in Modern Painters V, *Ruskin said: 'Nor can the character of any tree be known... until not only its branches, but its minutest extremities have been drawn...'*

3. JOHN RUSKIN

Childhood gardening

John Ruskin had loved gardens and gardening since childhood. His mother's chief personal pleasure, he tells the readers of his autobiography *Praeterita* (meaning 'things past') 'was in her flowers'. After he had finished his morning task of learning long passages from the Bible and, as he grew older, Latin grammar as well, he would go out into the garden of the family house at Herne Hill, where Mrs Ruskin was 'often planting or pruning beside me'. Later he wrote of this garden:

> The first joy of the year being in the snowdrops, the second, and cardinal one, was in the almond blossom, – every other garden and woodland gladness following from that in an unbroken order of kindling flower and shadowy leaf; and for many and many a year to come … my chief prayer for the kindness of heaven, in its flowerful seasons, was that the frost might not touch the almond blossom.

Wildness in plants

In his youth and for the rest of his life Ruskin scorned the conventional formal gardens of the nineteenth century, preferring instead the simple beauty of wild plants in wild places. Famously, early in his career, he wrote in *The Poetry of Architecture* (1837-8):

> A flower garden is an ugly thing, even when best managed: it is an assembly of unfortunate beings, pampered and bloated above their natural size, stewed and heated into diseased growth; corrupted by evil communication into speckled and inharmonious colours; torn from the soil which they loved, and of which they were the spirit and glory, to slave away their term of tormented life among the mixed and incongruous essences of each other, in earth that they know not, and in air that is poison to them.

For good measure, he went on to say:

> And the flower-garden is as ugly in effect as it is unnatural in feeling: it never will harmonise with anything, and if people will have it, should be kept out of sight till they get into it.

In contrast, the beauty of wild flowers, especially in their natural wild habitats, frequently

Margaret Ruskin (1781–1871), mother of John Ruskin, by James Northcote, R. A. (1825)

Opposite: John Ruskin's love of wildness is perfectly captured in his dramatic watercolour entitled Rocks and Ferns in a Wood, Crossmount, Perthshire, 1847, *to be seen at Abbot Hall Art Gallery, Kendal, Cumbria*

39

Oxalis, twice natural size. + sketch

Wood Sorrel (Oxalis acetosella) by John Ruskin. This delightful wild flower thrives in the woodland shade at Brantwood, but in John Ruskin's mind has particular associations with Chamonix in the French Alps and was described in his Diary for 4th February 1844 as his 'favourite Chamouni [sic] plant'. 'The triple leaf of this plant,' he wrote in Modern Painters *(1843), 'and white flower, stained purple, probably gave it strange typical interest among the Christian painters.' He wrote about his drawings of wood sorrel in* Proserpina *(1882), his eccentric book on botany. Emphasizing his belief that the flower of a plant is more important than the fruit, he notes of the wood sorrel that 'its entire function is decorative; it is virtually a flowering plant, - not one for either fruit or seed; its fruit is nothing, and the whole aim of Nature in it is to give the flower an infinite tenderness'*

moved him to write about them with great sensitivity and tenderness. In *Proserpina*, his controversial yet fascinating book on botany, significantly subtitled *Studies of Wayside Flowers …among the Alps, and in Scotland and England which my Father knew*, he wrote:

> I have in my hand a small red poppy… It is an intensely simple, intensely floral flower. All silk and flame: a scarlet cup…seen among the wild grass, far away, like a burning coal fallen from Heaven's altars. You cannot have a more complete, a more stainless, type of flower absolute… (*Proserpina*, 1882)

And elsewhere in the same work, with great botanical insight, he describes a weed as:

> A vegetable which has an innate disposition to get into the wrong place… It is not its being venomous, or ugly, but its being impertinent – thrusting itself where it has no business, and hinders other people's business – that makes a weed of it.

Ruskin loved to draw wild flowers as well as write about them, as he also tells the readers of the introduction to *Proserpina*, written at Brantwood in 1874:

> I had begun my studies of Alpine botany… in 1842, by making a careful drawing of wood-sorrel at Chamouni; and bitterly sorry I am, now, that the work was interrupted. For I drew, then, very delicately; and should have made a pretty book if I could have got peace. Even yet, I… would far rather be making outlines of flowers than writing; and I meant to have drawn every English and Scottish wild flower… back, and profile, and front.

Water and landscape

Until his move to Brantwood in 1872 there had been few opportunities for Ruskin to work out his ideas on gardening on a large canvas. There had been the gardens of the family homes at 28 Herne Hill and 163 Denmark Hill, of course, but he had simply watched or assisted his mother there. In *Praeterita* he describes a canal he wished to dig in the garden at Denmark Hill, where the family moved in 1842, but this came to nothing:

> … ever since first I could drive a spade, I had wanted to dig a canal, and make locks in it, like Harry in *Harry and Lucy* [a book by Maria Edgeworth]. And in the field at the back of the Denmark Hill house… I saw my way to a canal with any number of locks down towards Dulwich… [But] I never got my canal dug, after all!... I had never, till

now that the need came, entered into the statistics of water supply. The gardeners wanted all that was in the water butts for the greenhouse. Nothing but a dry ditch, incommodious to cows, I saw to be possible and resigned myself to destiny: yet the bewitching idea never went out of my head, and some water-works, on the model of Fontainebleau, were verily set aflowing – twenty years afterwards, as will be told.

Then, in a footnote, he refers the reader to the chapter entitled 'Joanna's Care', in which he describes how his cousin, Joan, or Joanna, Agnew (the future Mrs Severn) came from Scotland to look after his mother in her declining years. Towards the end of this chapter he wrote, in 1889:

I draw back to my own home [probably Denmark Hill], twenty years ago, permitted to thank Heaven once more for the peace, and hope, and loveliness of it, and the Elysian walks with Joanie, and Paradisical with Rosie [La Touche], under the peach blossom branches by the little glittering stream which I had paved with crystal for them. I had built behind the highest cluster of laurels, a reservoir, from which, on sunny afternoons, I could let a quite rippling film of water run for a couple of hours down behind the hay-field, where the grass in spring still grew fresh and deep. There used to be a corncrake in it… and the little stream had its falls, and pools, and imaginary lakes. Here and there it laid for itself lines of graceful sand; there and here it lost

The garden at 28 Herne Hill, John Ruskin's childhood home It was here that the young boy first acquired from his mother a deep love of flowers. The small black ink sketch is by Arthur Severn and was made between 1871 and 1900

41

itself under beads of chalcedony. It wasn't the Liffey nor the Nith, nor the Wandel; but the two girls were surely a little cruel to call it 'The Gutter'.

Such preoccupation with 'landscape gardening', especially the management of water, was to re-emerge in his gardening at Brantwood, but the landscapes and plants at Herne Hill and Denmark Hill could hardly be called 'wild', with the exception, perhaps, of the large meadow where the corncrake dwelt. He had bought land in Chamonix in 1863, but had done nothing with it. And although he had contributed to *The Garden*, the magazine edited by the celebrated nineteenth-century populariser of gardening with wild plants, William Robinson, it was mainly on social rather than horticultural matters.

He had, however, observed wild plants in their native habitats during his extensive travels, especially in Scotland, Italy and the Alps and had written about them and drawn them, equally extensively, in *Modern Painters* (especially Volumes III and V) and in his Diaries and notebooks.

Brantwood: a 'living laboratory'

At Brantwood he found for the first time his own landscape to work on. Moreover, it was a landscape shaped by the hand of man over the centuries, with much evidence of its long association with people still visible, despite having been reclaimed by nature. All this would have appealed to Ruskin and so he set to with a will, doing much of the manual work himself, assisted in the early stages by his head gardener David Downes, whom he had brought with him from London, and later by Dawson Herdson. Downes left Brantwood in the late 1870s to manage the Guild of St George's farm at Totley, Sheffield and was succeeded as head gardener by Herdson, who had probably worked at Brantwood since 1871. Visitors were also pressed into service to help with particular projects. For example, two Oxford undergraduates (one of them his future biographer W. G. Collingwood) staying at Brantwood in the long vacation of 1875 to help with the translation of Xenophon's *Economist*, were recruited to help with the deepening and enlargement of the harbour. Over the next thirteen to fourteen years paths and steps were cut through the woods, vistas opened up, streams bridged, dammed or diverted and islands of cultivated garden created. In carrying out these projects, Ruskin always combined some practical social or intellectual experimentation with the desire to create an aesthetically pleasing effect. Moreover, he always stressed the importance of the garden as an educational resource for self-improvement, writing to a young lady reader of *Fors Clavigera – Letters to the Workmen and Labourers of Great Britain*, in 1874, for example:

John Ruskin in 1885, sturdy rustic walking stick in hand, resting against the dry-stone wall of the north drive at Brantwood. The moist air of Lakeland has encouraged a rich flora of mosses, ferns and other plants to thrive in the spaces between the stones

> Your garden is to enable you to obtain such knowledge… as you may best use in the country in which you live by communicating it to others; and teaching them to take pleasure in the green herb, given for meat, and the coloured flower given for joy.

Collingwood tells us that:

> …though he loved to see flowers (especially wild ones) on his table and outside his window, yet in his practical gardening [he] was quite the landscapist. He liked making paths and contriving pretty nooks, building steps and bridges, laying out beds, woodcutting and so forth; but I never remember him potting and grafting and layering and budding…

His was not, however, the formal, structured hard landscaping of the professional garden maker. Rather, he always followed the grain of the land and worked with local materials – especially wood and slate. His steps were always uneven, with plants growing in the cracks, his paths were never straight (although they always led somewhere) and his bridges were rough-hewn. According to Collingwood his plants were invariably wild species (especially in the wooded areas) or old-fashioned varieties:

> …and as to the rarity of any plant in his garden, I believe he took far more pleasure

44

in the wood-anemone — Silvia, he called it — than in anything buyable from the nurseryman's catalogue.

Despite all this informality, however, therein lies a paradox, for although Ruskin loved wildness in plants, so far as his gardens were concerned it had to be a wildness shaped to his own design, albeit a design that resulted from a 'conversation' with the landscape and flora, rather than simply being imposed upon them. Moreover, although Ruskin took great pleasure in such British native wild plants as the wood anemone, it may be conjectured that his gardens probably also had to include plants that were wild natives of places he had visited in mainland Europe, especially the Alps — wild daffodils, for example — for his writings about plants, notably *Proserpina*, include frequent references to the association of particular wild plants with 'memories' of special places.

The influence of Botticelli

Probably one of Ruskin's most far-reaching changes at Brantwood was that he would not allow the coppice to be cut any more, letting the trees grow up and only taking out the weaker shoots and dead wood. In Collingwood's words:

> ...[the coppice] spindled up to great tall stems, slender and sinuous, promising no timber and past the age for all commercial use or time-honoured wont. Neighbours shook their heads, but [unlike Ruskin] they did not know the pictures of Botticelli…

Ascent to the Heaven of Fire: *illustration of c. 1490 by Sandro Botticelli (1445–1510) for the first canto of Paradiso, part of Dante's* Divine Comedy. *It shows Dante and Beatrice ascending from the earthly paradise of Eden, their last point of contact with the earth*

Ruskin had made his coppice into the background of an early Italian painting in which one would not be surprised to see a goddess appear out of the green depths, with the blue of the lake and the dark blue of the mountains just visible to the west through the sun-dappled foliage. Collingwood goes on to tell us that:

> [To keep his] forest at this delightful point of mystery, his bill-hook and gloves were always lying on the hall table.

> After writing in the morning he would go up to the wood and chop away until lunch time. This was not … heroic axe-work …, but such pruning as a Garden of Eden required to dress it and to keep it.

Ironically, the abandonment of coppicing by Ruskin would have slowly resulted in a deepening of the shade in the woodland and, as a result, the gradual suppression of the wild woodland plants he loved so much.

45

4. JOHN RUSKIN'S GARDENS

Six of John Ruskin's garden projects, in various stages of restoration or renovation – 'being brought back to life for a modern audience', as Sally Beamish says – may be seen at Brantwood today: the Professor's Garden (Ruskin's favourite); the Painter's Glade (once also a tennis court); the Precipice Path; the Pond; Zig-zaggy; and the Moorland Garden. Each will be discussed in detail, together with diversions to consider Ruskin's Seat, his Ice House and the former Kitchen Garden. Some of the plants of interest to be seen in each garden throughout the year are listed on pp. 115-118.

The Professor's Garden (from 1872 onwards)

In 1870 Ruskin became the Slade Professor of Fine Art at the University of Oxford, a post he held for the rest of the decade, hence the name given affectionately by family and local people to his own 'special' garden.

He wrote in a letter to a friend soon after acquiring Brantwood:

> I am at work in my little garden amongst the hills conscious of little more than the dust of the earth, more at peace than of old…

And in his diary for September 15th 1871 he wrote:

> Heavenly walk by stream in the morning. First day's work at clearing garden. See weeds burnt in the twilight.

Collingwood describes the garden as being in the heart of the wood, approached by a true woodland path – not gravelled – with rough steps of local slate, and ferns and saxifrages growing in the cracks. It was about as large as a cottager's kitchen garden, fenced on two sides with wooden paling, with an old stone wall, mossy and ivied, keeping off the trees and undergrowth on the higher side of the hill.

The fourth side of this private paradise had no fence, being separated from the woodland by a steep beck, flowing and on occasions tumbling, in all but the driest weather (a rare event at Brantwood), in a series of cascades over the hard slate rocks that formed

Opposite: The Professor's Garden with its restored 'penthouse' in late spring. Ruskin kept bees here, and the space beneath the stone shelf has been arranged to encourage them today. The old rose 'The Garland', bred in 1835, now scrambles over the roof of the penthouse, while Geranium 'Ann Folkard' (a hybrid of G. procurrens x G. psilostemon) dominates the foreground

its bed. Stones were continually washed down from above and Ruskin sometimes complained, light-heartedly, of the difficulty of keeping the beck clear, drawing attention to the geological lessons to be learned from a stream that continually filled rather than deepened its bed.

The gate to the Professor's Garden in Ruskin's time

Ruskin's special garden was probably adapted from the 'small garden' referred to by Linton in his *Memories* of 1894 (see p. 21). As a working garden, this limited area of ground provided Ruskin with the peace and tranquillity he desperately needed and an opportunity to experiment with the cultivation and display of wild and cultivated, ornamental and edible, plants on challenging land. He alone planned and managed this garden. Here he grew flowers, fruit and herbs suitable for a local cottager's garden, choosing to arrange them in such a way as to provide examples of the cultivation of food for the souls, as well as the bodies, of the local labourers.

Ruskin's arrival at Brantwood coincided with his founding of the Guild of St. George, through which he hoped to encourage the purchase of derelict land by public donation, to be reclaimed and cultivated by tenants in sympathy with their surroundings. The Brantwood estate may have become, in Ruskin's mind, one such experiment, with himself as both master and tenant, and his special garden is where he started.

Ruskin himself made very few specific records of his plantings, his gardens being places for the exploration of ideas that were later published in books and pamphlets, rather than being written up for their own sake. It is mainly thanks to Collingwood, therefore, that we can determine what Ruskin actually grew in his garden. He had 'an espalier of apples and a little gooseberry patch and a few standard fruit-trees', Collingwood says, 'and some strawberries mixed with flowers'. Moreover, in one corner 'there were beehives in an old-fashioned penthouse, trailed over with creepers'.

Opposite: A peaceful corner of the Professor's Garden in early summer. In the centre is a drift of the blue-flowered perennial cornflower (Centaurea montana), a typical cottage garden plant

After Ruskin's last illness, in 1888, the Professor's Garden was abandoned and returned to nature until its renovation in the early 1990s. It is approached from near to the house by rough steps and a narrow woodland path. On passing through the simple wooden gate at the end of the path the visitor enters a private world that is still much as Collingwood described it, thanks to careful restoration by Sally Beamish and her team. The walls and fences have been repaired and the penthouse, now covered by a rambling rose ('The Garland'), has been largely rebuilt, for the roof and upper parts had disappeared and the base buried under rubbly soil. Ruskin's straw bee-skeps have gone, of course, leaving only the stone shelf that supported them as a rudimentary seat from which the visitor may admire the garden even on the rainiest of days. The bees have

Rhododendron petal. This pencil sketch, made at Brantwood, is an example of Ruskin 'seeing through drawing' in his botanical studies. It is inscribed in brown ink: ' Spots on Rhododendron petal – Brantwood main garden. To show principle of <u>order</u> in pardonable <u>disorder</u>.'

Opposite: Blossom of an espalier-trained apple tree at Brantwood. Ruskin's voice can almost be heard, insisting that: 'The flower exists for its own sake,— not for the fruit's sake. The production of the fruit is an added honour to it—is a granted consolation to us for its death.'
Proserpina, *Volume I*

not vanished, however, for the space below the shelf is filled with innumerable pieces of hollow, dried stems of various diameters that provide homes for the many benign bumble- bees and hoverflies that abound in the garden. Such a diversity of pollinating insects is a clear indication of the overall 'health' of the plot.

The espalier-trained fruit trees, which have replaced those lost from Ruskin's time, were planted in c. 1990. All are old apple varieties suitable for the cool wet climate of north-west England (see opposite).

The pink blossom in spring is likely to have been Ruskin's principal reason for including such trees in his garden, for as he says in *Praeterita*:

> …very early indeed in my thoughts of trees, I had got at the principle given fifty years afterwards in 'Proserpina', that the seeds and fruits of them were for the sake of the flowers, not the flowers for the fruit.

No doubt, however, the autumn fruits would have provided both an aesthetic and a culinary bonus, as they do today.

The rest of the garden is now planted with a mixture of annual and perennial herbs, vegetables and wild and old-fashioned garden flowers, apparently all mixed together, as one might expect in a cottager's garden. This jumble is not all that it seems, however, and deserves close examination, for considerable care has been exercised by its planner, Dave Charles, in the true spirit of Ruskin, in devising the content of the beds. The whole garden is managed on organic principles, without the use of artificial fertilizers or pesticides, with much attention being devoted to the flowering times, colours, shapes and forms of the naturally slug- and snail-resistant plants. This ensures a continuous, aesthetically harmonious and productive display throughout the seasons that is also attractive to bees, butterflies and other wildlife.

One may leave the tranquillity of the Professor's Garden by a lower or an upper route. The lower one leads over a simple wooden bridge that crosses the beck. Collingwood writes of this bridge as follows.

> It [the beck] was crossed by a rough wooden bridge. I remember at the building of this bridge he [Ruskin] was considerably annoyed because the workman, thinking to please him with unusually rude lines, had made the planks so flimsy that it was hardly safe. He insisted on solidity and security, though his stone steps were so irregular as

ESPALIER-TRAINED APPLE VARIETIES PLANTED IN THE PROFESSOR'S GARDEN

* Descriptions based on information published by the National Fruit Collection, University of Reading.

Dessert varieties (listed from the bee shelter end of the garden)

White Transparent: Introduced to Western Europe, from Russia or the Baltic States, in the mid-1800s (also doubles as a cooking apple).

American Mother: Originated in Boston, Massachusetts, USA and first recorded in 1844.

Ribston Pippin: Raised at Ribston Hall, Yorkshire, from seed brought from Rouen, France and planted in 1707.

Pitmaston Pine Apple: Raised by Mr White, steward to Lord Foley, at Witley in *c.* 1785.

Cornish Aromatic: Originally found growing in Cornwall and first brought to notice in 1813, but thought to be many centuries old.

Brownlee's Russet: Raised in England and first introduced commercially in 1848.

Roundway Magnum Bonum: Raised by Mr Joy, gardener at Roundway Park, Devizes, Wiltshire, England and introduced in *c.* 1864.

Cooking varieties (listed from the bee shelter end of the garden)

Norfolk Beefing: Raised in Norfolk, England and first recorded in 1807.

Smart's Prince Arthur: Raised by Smart, near Sittingbourne, Kent, England and first described in 1883.

Lord Derby: Raised by Witham, Stockport, Cheshire, England and first recorded in 1862.

Belle de Boskoop: A triploid variety, thought to be a bud sport of Reinette de Montfort and found by R. J. W. Boskoop of the Netherlands in 1856.

French Crab: Thought to have originated in France and brought to England in the late 1700s.

Lane's Prince Albert: Thought to have been raised by Thomas Squire of Berkhamsted, England in *c.* 1840; introduced commercially in 1850.

Golden Noble: Discovered by Patrick Flanagan, head gardener to Sir Thomas Harr of Stowe Hall, Downham, Norfolk, England; mentioned by William Forsyth in 1803 and introduced to the Royal Horticultural Society in 1820.

The simple wooden bridge that crosses the beck beyond the Professor's Garden. The white flowers of aconite-leaf buttercup (Ranunculus aconitifolius) make a spectacular show in the spring sunshine

Oxlips flowering in spring, as they may be seen from Ruskin's Seat. In fact, these flowers are probably of false oxlip (Primula x polyantha), a natural hybrid of primrose and cowslip, since the true oxlip (Primula elatior) normally occurs only in eastern England

to contradict all the rules which bid you make stairs in a flight equal, for fear of tripping your passenger.

The bridge today is a new one and although 'rough', it is by no means flimsy. After crossing it, the visitor may either follow the path, which curves downwards towards the Painter's Glade (see p. 55), or turn left and climb a steep flight of slate steps that are as irregular as in Ruskin's day. These lead up beside the beck to Ruskin's Seat.

The upper route also leads to Ruskin's Seat – this way out is reached by stone steps beside the penthouse, which lead to a path along a terrace that looks down on the Professor's Garden and ends with a simple, additional 'clapper' bridge over the beck, made from a single flat piece of slate. The border beside the terrace path is planted with a diversity of flowering plants and vegetables, chosen and positioned each year so as to explore various themes. Amongst those explored so far are: organic insect control; organic slug and snail control; growing vegetables in local waste materials such as bracken; growing climbing vegetables over hazel arches; and creating a Cumbrian 'grow-bag' for potatoes using sheeps' fleece layered inside raised hurdles.

Beyond the bridge a few rough, uneven slate steps to the left lead to Ruskin's Seat itself, after which the path climbs for a while before descending above the Painter's Glade to the 'High Walk', one of Joan Severn's Gardens (see p. 79).

Ruskin's Seat: a great throne of riven slate from which to observe the beautiful complexity of the natural world

Ruskin's Seat (1874)

Ruskin's Seat is a substantial 'throne', built for Ruskin to sit and watch the tumbling waters of the beck. The story goes that while strolling in the garden of his friend and correspondent Susanna Beever, across the lake at The Thwaite, in 1874, Ruskin had happened upon and admired her 'two deeply interesting thrones of the ancient Abbotts of Furness'. The story continues that she subsequently sent her gardener to Brantwood to build a suitable throne for Ruskin near the beck, from where he could enjoy the sound of the rushing waters, admire the beauty of the ferns, primulas and other plants at the water's edge and study the geology of the cataract to his heart's content.

Today this massive seat, made from great slabs of riven slate in the form of a throne, leans backwards a little drunkenly into the trees, and is encrusted with numerous coloured lichens that thrive in the moist, clean air of the wood. Sitting in it now, quietly, in the shade of the trees, with only the sound of rustling leaves, birdsong and rushing water, it is not difficult to imagine what it must have been like for the great man to sit there after a hard day of writing and simply let his mind range free in contemplation of the wonders of nature – 'God's own creation'.

The Painter's Glade (1879)

Collingwood tells us that, once over the wooden bridge, the visitor would find in the wood, as now, frequent 'hummocks and bosses of rock pushing through the soil… each with its special interest of fern or flower'. Ruskin would lead the way, pointing out trails of ivy, clumps of moss and other wild plants, much as a conventional gardener might point out a prize orchid or other exotic. Convolvulus would not be seen, however, for this was always removed for fear of strangling the stems of less aggressive species.

Then, coming out of the wood, the visitor would come upon the tennis lawn, which, Collingwood says, was a concession to youthful visitors to Brantwood, for Ruskin had no interest in athletic pursuits. Nevertheless, he took the keenest interest in the creation of this glade, believing in 'diggings of all sorts', and acted as engineer and foreman, the work itself being done by the young people who were eventually to use the lawn for its intended purpose. Thus in June 1879, Ruskin's Diary informs us, guests and gardeners were grubbing out tree roots to create the tennis court, although the impractical Ruskin, intending to be helpful, had rendered their task more difficult by cutting the trees down first, with the result that the workers had no leverage for pulling up the roots.

Once the tennis lawn was complete, the saplings around it grew tall, creating on one side a 'veil' through which the lake might be viewed, while on the other side they formed a shady prelude to the dark wooded hill above. Collingwood says that:

> … it has a curious touch of poetry. There is no statue on a pedestal or fountain playing in a basin, but on the mossy bank, beneath the graceful lines of virginal forestry, Decamerons might have been told. It is an oasis in this North-country farmer's neighbourhood… [Only Ruskin could have turned something so utilitarian as] a tennis-ground into a Purist painter's glade.

The glade is little different today. The trees surrounding it are certainly higher, although perhaps less dense, the undergrowth of a century of neglect has been removed, the grass of the lawn has largely been replaced by mosses and leafy liverworts, and a contemporary willow-screen sculpture reflecting the distant fells has until recently (soon to be reinstated) provided a foreground to the lake. Around the edge in spring are clumps of native *Narcissus* hybrids and here and there in the dark wood may be seen a flash of colour in spring or autumn in the form of a flowering *Rhododendron*, *Azalea* or *Pieris*. But the glade is still a cool, green oasis and still retains its touch of poetry and mystery. It is to the great credit of Sally Beamish and her staff that they have had the wisdom to let well alone, for this is a place to rest, to dream and to lose all sense of time.

Opposite: The Painter's Glade, once intended as a tennis court, but now a peaceful oasis of green tranquillity. The grassy playing surface was long ago replaced by moss, which thrives in the shade of the trees and creates a soft springy carpet that is a joy to walk on. The willow screen on the western edge of the glade reflects the shape of the Coniston fells beyond the lake

55

The Precipice Path (1879)

Upon leaving the Painter's Glade at its far southern end, if one turns immediately left for a few yards on the path leading back to Ruskin's Seat, there to the right is another precipitous flight of Ruskin's characteristically uneven stone steps, recently uncovered, snaking their way up the wooded hillside.

Ruskin's Diary for March 23rd 1879 reads:

> Yesterday making the path up under the 'precipice rock'. I must find some less grand name.

And for 22nd April of the same year:

> Joanie [Joan Severn], on Saturday, completed the planting of my lovely little garden of Hyacinth [bluebell] and [wood] Anemone under my 'precipice rock.'

If one climbs the steps, there at the top, just below the dry-stone boundary wall, is a large rocky outcrop, forming a miniature cliff or precipice, reminiscent of outcrops in the Alps or the mountains of Scotland. Beneath it the scrub and undergrowth have been removed from the area where the hyacinths and anemones must once have bloomed. Mosses and ferns are now there in abundance but soon the area will have been replanted to bloom again in spring, as Ruskin intended.

Beyond the precipice rock, the path climbs close to the boundary wall and then descends around the shoulder of the hill towards the Pond.

On a snowy January morning in 2013 Sally Beamish contemplates the replanting of the bed beneath the 'precipice rock', as Ruskin called the picturesque rocky outcrop at the top of the Precipice Path. Soon, it is hoped, bluebells and wood anemones will bloom here again, as Ruskin originally intended

Ruskin's Pond in spring, the surrounding woodland floor carpeted with bluebells and ferns. Throughout the year the pond appears as an almost circular mirror reflecting the sky and the trees

Ruskin's Pond: the wooden sluice that made it possible for the outflow to be regulated at will

The Pond (probably conceived in 1874 but not completed until c.1877-8)

Although the Pond may be approached from the track leading south from the Painter's Glade, the finest view of it is undoubtedly the one from the high point just beyond the Precipice Path. Here in winter and spring, before the leaves are on the trees and providing there is no wind, it appears as an almost circular mirror, reflecting the sky, the tall stems of the trees surrounding it and, in spring, the carpet of bluebells beneath them, 'guiding the eye off the land with the reflection', just as Ruskin intended.

First mentioned by Ruskin in 1874, his pond was probably not completed until c. 1877-8. It may originally have been intended simply as a fishpond and reflecting surface, but possibly later became a place for studying fish. It is carefully placed so that it can be fed by water from a small natural stream that rises on the hill above, and this has recently been canalized with stone as it approaches the pond itself. Moreover, water flowing out of the pond on the opposite side from the stream could easily be controlled by a small wooden sluice that drained down the hill. Thus it would have been possible to regulate the level and the through-put of water, or to drain the pond completely, if required – all essential attributes of an experimental reservoir. As with all Ruskin's experimental garden projects, however, it is most probable that the aesthetic, reflecting qualities of his creation, as well as its technical features, were in the forefront of his mind from the outset.

The pond today contains no fish, although its aesthetic qualities remain and continue to delight the eye. It provides a haven for myriads of water-dependent insects, but there are fewer frogs and newts than in the past, for although spawn is sometimes seen, this is usually now eaten by visiting mallards. Native and exotic ferns have been planted around the pond, including the handsome yet delicate Royal Fern *(Osmunda regalis)*.

Common polypody (Polypodium vulgare), a wintergreen native fern that may be seen throughout the woodland at Brantwood

Zig-zaggy: preliminary sketches of the zig-zag path in a letter from John Ruskin to Joan Severn dated March 1873. Ruskin writes in the baby language which he and Joan sometimes used between themselves: 'Me can't draw it di ma [his pet name for Joan] – me's blotted it so – there's a steep walk up the middle, with steps at the terraces – and the terraces zigzag, and [the scribbled area] is Brantwood.' Then he describes a visit to [Alfie], who everybody says is 'so good', and there's so much to do he can't do it on his own. The letter is signed Di Pa [Ruskin's own pet name]. The postscript mentions his pleasure in the primroses, and in going out at 6.00 am, when 'everything looked as if it were in Parrydise [sic]'. The centre path was probably never built and is not part of the restoration

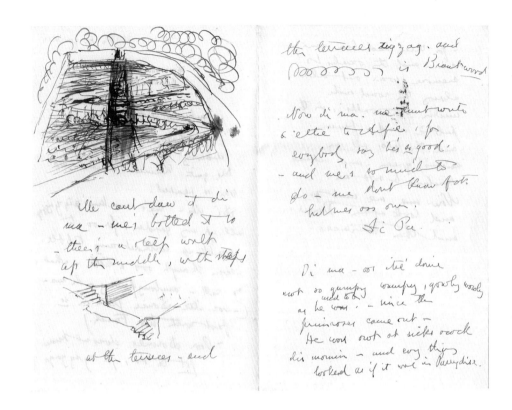

Zig-zaggy (1873)

A Heritage Lottery Fund grant of £50,000 (2001-03) made possible the renovation and restoration of the southern gardens, from Zig-zaggy to the High Walk (see p. 79).

Zig-zaggy, a most fascinating garden, is best approached from the somewhat prosaic environs of the present-day car park, an area once occupied by a kitchen garden (see p. 70). Designed in 1873, soon after Ruskin's move to Brantwood, it exemplifies the way in which he incorporated different ideas into a single project.

Inspired by his observations of mountain farming in northern Italy to experiment at Brantwood with the growing of plants on steep ground, Ruskin created a series of terraces, retained by simple, uncapped walls made from local stones found on the land, with

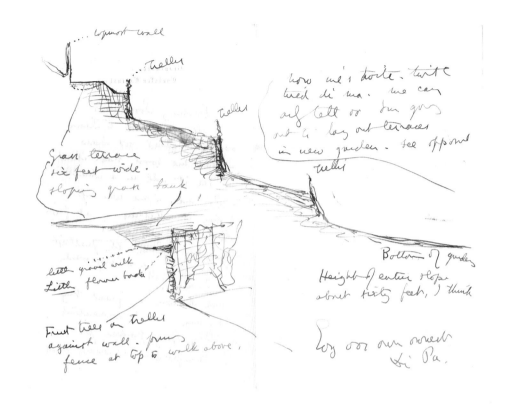

a path zig-zagging up between them. Collingwood writes of these terraces as:

> Hedged with apple and the cotoneaster which flourishes at Coniston, and filled in with sloping patches of strawberry and gooseberry… This irregularity and cottage garden business would have offended those new-comers who buy a bit of nature at the Lakes and improve away all its beauties.

Writing to his cousin Joan Severn about his ideas for this part of the garden, Ruskin carefully described the zig-zag path between the terraces, which he illustrated with two small sketches. Moreover, according to Collingwood, Ruskin later set out to create in his Moorland Garden, higher up the hill: 'a paradise of terraces like the top of the purgatorial mount in Dante'. Thus the structure of the whole hillside at Brantwood may have been intended to reflect the form of Dante's 'Purgatorial Mount', with the summit of the

Zig-zaggy

Gundula Deutschlander, a former member of the garden staff, who played a major part in the Zig-zaggy restoration

Opposite: Lust – garish red lips with a house-leek (Sempervivum) tongue tempt the visitor in Sally Beamish's planting of Zig-zaggy as a representation of the 'seven deadly sins'

Mount near the top of the hill represented by the Paradise Terraces of the Moorland Garden, and the early approaches to it represented by the zig-zag path winding up between the terraces above the car-park.

Having collapsed and become buried beneath trees and undergrowth during the ninety years following Ruskin's death, the zig-zag path and its rotting stone terraces were re-discovered by Sally Beamish and her volunteers in the early 1990s. Grant funding in 2001 enabled the extraordinary site to live again, providing the opportunity to re-create, using contemporary plantings and landscape detailing, the complex imagery of the Purgatorial Mount. Thus Sally Beamish writes:

> On entering the garden, imagine leaving Hell and beginning a journey upwards to cleanse your soul. The structure and colours within the terrace beds represent the seven deadly sins of Pride, Envy, Wrath, Sloth, Avarice, Gluttony and Lust. Appreciate your stay in Purgatory, but remember you are there to reflect and repent, not to enjoy yourself.

> The planting of this garden also exemplifies a key Ruskin belief, namely that 'the greatest thing a human soul ever does in this world is to see clearly'. You may enjoy the effect of the plants at their face value, or for their symbolism, but many will repay closer contemplation, both of themselves and of how they relate to their fellows. Ruskin knew that much could be learnt from the world around us by looking long and hard at its humblest details.

At the top of Zig-zaggy, the path provides an alternative route through the woods to the green oasis of the Painter's Glade, already described, and a return to more pagan imagery, as Collingwood writes of the trees in the wood following Ruskin's cessation of coppicing:

> ... among those slender-pillared aisles you would not be surprised to see goddesses appear out of the green depths; and looking westwards, the sun-dazzle of the lake and the dark blue of the mountains gazed in between the leaves.

Sally Beamish remarks that 'visitors are advised not to be tempted to retrace their steps and descend through Purgatory as this may lead to eternal damnation'.

PRIDE

Acanthus spinosus bear's breeches
Allium karataviense onion
Cynara cardunculus cardoon
Crambe maritima sea kale
Datisca cannabina
Euphorbia mellifera honey spurge
Gunnera magellanica
Hosta sieboldiana var. *elegans* plantain lily
Leucanthemella serotina
Paeonia lutea yellow tree peony
Papaver orientale oriental poppy
Phormium 'Sunset'
Rheum palmatum 'Atropurpureum'
    ornamental rhubarb
Rodgersia podophylla
Zantedeschia aethiopica arum lily

ENVY

Celmisia semicordata New Zealand daisy
Corokia cotoneaster wire-netting bush
Eryngium variifolium sea holly
Eryngium bourgatii
Dipsacus laciniata teasel

AVARICE

Blechnum spicant hard fern
Potentilla eriocarpa
Alchemilla erythropoda red-stemmed
    lady's mantle
Lysimachia nemorum yellow pimpernel
Primula veris cowslip

WRATH

Carex comans bronze-leaved sedge
Carex muskingumensis palm branch sedge

Festuca amethystina
Hakonechloa macra 'Aureola'
Miscanthus sinensis 'Silberfeder' silver feather
Molinia caerulea 'Transparent' purple moor
    grass
Stipa gigantea giant feather grass,
    golden oats

SLOTH

Allium schoenoprasum chives
Armeria maritima sea thrift
Astelia nervosa 'Westland'
Crocosmia masonorum Montbretia
Diplarrena moraea
Eucomis bicolor pineapple flower
Eryngium agavifolium
Hemerocallis 'Pink Damask' daylily
Kniphofia caulescens red hot poker
Lilium pyrenaicum Bowle's golden grass
Muscari armeniacum 'Fantasy Creation'
    grape hyacinth
Nectaroscordum siculum subsp. *bulgaricum*
Ophiopogon planiscapus 'Nigrescens' lilyturf
Hesperantha coccinea 'Major' kaffir lily
Camassia cusickii

GLUTTONY

Pyrus communis 'Jargonelle' pear
Pyracantha 'Dart's Red'/'Interrada' firethorn
Pyrus communis 'Black Worcester' pear

LUST

Imperata cylindrica 'Red Baron' Japanese
    blood grass
Phormium 'Sunset'
Sempervivum tectorum houseleek

John Ruskin's silhouette (detail) of himself leading a working party to high ground on the estate, probably on 15th September 1881, the year in which he began thinking about cultivating the highest parts of the hill behind the house

Opposite: the Moorland Garden in an oil painting by W. G. Collingwood entitled 'Professor Ruskin's Orchard, Brantwood 1904 – A scene of the Moorland Garden from the bridleway above with Coniston and the fells beyond'

The Moorland Garden (1881)

This garden is found by turning left near the old front door of the house and following the path through the Fern Garden (see p. 93) to an old iron gate in the dry-stone boundary wall. Through this, by ascending further, the visitor reaches the open land higher up the hill.

Collingwood writes:

> It was in the late 'seventies, when the first illness had forced him to spend most of his time at Brantwood, and in the early 'eighties, before final illness put an end to his activity, that Ruskin… went higher up the hill for new worlds to conquer. His bit of moor above the wood was opened out into a new sort of garden, quite as charming in its way as any other.

In fact, Ruskin began to think about cultivating the highest parts of the hill behind the House towards the end of 1881. Here he created his Moorland Garden and on 25th October he informed Joan Severn that he had two of the local builder's men and other helpers 'all in full force on the bit of ground and it is really coming into force fast'. This 'bit of ground' was a steep area of hillside overlooking Coniston Water, with a foreground of woodland foliage and the mountains above as a background. It had already been cleared of the wild growth of oak, birch and holly by the charcoal burners and farmers in the preceding centuries, and according to Collingwood:

> Strongly marked ridges of slate-rock cropped out slantwise, across and across the slope, their backs tufted with heather and juniper, and their hollows holding water in sodden quagmires.

Ruskin might simply have drained this intake of ground and put it down to grass, as a farmer would have done, but such an action was anathema to him, for it would have destroyed the inherent beauty and charm of the moorland. So (Collingwood again):

> Just as a portrait-painter studies to pose his sitter in such a light and in such an attitude as to bring out the most individual points and get the revelation of a personality, so Ruskin studied his moor, to develop its resources.

After this contemplation of the ground, Ruskin embarked upon a novel experiment in upland agriculture. It was the last of his great practical schemes and although continuing

'The Waterfall at Brantwood Door' *in a painting by Laurence Hilliard, reproduced in* W. G. Collingwood's book Ruskin Relics *(1903). This was the waterfall fed from the two reservoirs in the Moorland Garden that could be turned on and off as Ruskin directed*

Opposite: The edge of the Moorland Garden, with a weed-choked reservoir, in the depths of winter

for only a few years, the original concept for this garden still testifies today to the visionary nature of much of Ruskin's work. Located about 150 metres above sea-level, the site presented Ruskin with many challenges. From a piece of rough, boggy moorland he wished to create a carefully managed plot where the main strengths of the natural site and its vegetation supported and enhanced the cultivation of the less favoured ground. He first marshalled his staff and his visitors into a work-force (they called themselves the 'Board of Works') to drain the site by exposing the bedrock and allowing this to guide the water from two streams into what he hoped would be two sturdy reservoirs, to provide irrigation for the crops he intended to grow. These would then drain into a single stream to feed a waterfall near the house that could be turned on and off whenever required (there is an echo here of Ruskin's earlier attempts to create waterworks at Denmark Hill).

When the basins of the two reservoirs at Brantwood were completed, however, it was found that the earth banks were of insufficient strength to hold the water, which quickly drained away. Skilled labour had to be called in to build new dams of stone and mortar that were less attractive, but far more efficient, than the earth of the originals. Turning a necessity into a virtue, however, Collingwood tells us that Ruskin devised sluices with clever gates and artistically curved long-lever handles with which to open or close the drainage slits.

> And after his reservoirs were made, it was a favourite entertainment to send up somebody to turn the water on and produce a roaring cascade among the laurels opposite the front door [of the house].

A subsequent refinement of the scheme was that an enormous underground reservoir to store water from the Moorland Garden was blasted out of the rock, just below the boundary wall, and roofed over with lengths of railway track supporting slate slabs. Water was then diverted via a pipe from this chamber to feed an existing, smaller underground cistern above the house, to enhance Brantwood's domestic water supply.

With the drainage and irrigation of the site sorted out, Ruskin next had to clear the selected cultivation areas, and trial his chosen crops. Juniper, or savin-bush as it was known locally, was rooted out all over the site, for Ruskin hated it, just as he hated *Convolvulus* in the wood. The heather (ling – *Calluna vulgaris*) and heaths *(Erica)* were cherished, however, and the local custom of periodically burning the 'heather' to encourage the growth of grass resisted, so that 'the natural garden of ling and bell heather [*Erica cinerea*] might thrive'.

Cherry trees blossoming on one of the terraces of 'Ruskin's Moorland Garden' – an illustration by W. G. Collingwood in his book Ruskin Relics *(1903)*

Next the areas to be cropped were terraced, the stones for rough walls to retain the soil being gathered from the surrounding area. Collingwood says that one particularly wet patch was planted with cranberries, and apple and cherry trees planted where the ground was sufficiently deep and well drained to accommodate them. But neither the fruits of these trees, nor the other crops such as hardy wheat varieties that Ruskin perhaps hoped to grow in his Moorland Garden, were ever harvested for, as Collingwood remarks:

> …since this fragment of an experiment was completed , when strength no longer allowed him to stride up to this once favourite height, the whole has been left to Nature again. The apple-trees grew, but untended… the cherries have run wild and are left to the birds. The rough stone steps from the rock platform to the orchard terrace are disjointed and fern is creeping through the grass.
>
> > But yet from out the little hill
> > Oozes the slender streamlet still,
>
> …and perhaps it may – for no one can foretell the fate of any sacred spot – when the pilgrim of the future tries to identify by its help alone the whereabouts of Ruskin's deserted garden.

When Sally Beamish arrived and did indeed identify the whereabouts of the Moorland Garden and Ruskin's other gardens, she was faced with a challenge:

> How should we proceed to take a piece of living landscape, with such visionary potential, into the twenty-first century? Should we leave it untouched, as testimony to Ruskin's unfinished vision? Should we restore it, repairing the reservoirs, walls and terraces and making the water flow again? Should we continue the experiment where Ruskin left off, by growing fruit and trying to establish a hardy wheat variety, or should we take the philosophy of Ruskin's work and apply it to our own time?
>
> To date, we have begun to restore the basic structure of the old garden, as Ruskin knew it. But for the present it will remain, simply presented, as a blank canvas – as a place of questions, not of crops.

And long may it remain so, for the Moorland Garden is for me the most atmospheric of the gardens at Brantwood, especially in winter, with Ruskin's restless spirit seeming always to be at one's side.

Opposite: the 'blank canvas' of the Moorland Garden slowly greening in early spring

During the 1870s Ruskin always hired a carriage, when he needed one, from the Waterhead Hotel at the head of the lake. Between 1881 and 1882, however, he embarked on a plan, with Joan Severn, to build for the family a coach house, complete with stables behind. This was a huge job and involved blasting out and carting away about a hundred tons of white clay 'before we can ask what next!' Once the job was completed, the small area of land immediately below (now occupied by the car-park) was developed as an extra kitchen garden to feed the growing household. The cultivation of vegetables in due season, for home consumption, was dear to Ruskin's heart, as is apparent from his writings about the purposes of the Guild of St George and in the following specific advice given to a young lady correspondent in 1874:

> The use of your garden to the household ought to be mainly in the vegetables you can raise in it. And, for these, your proper observance of season, and of the authority of the stars, is a vital duty. Every climate gives its vegetable food to its living creatures at the right time; your business is to know that time, and to be prepared for it, and to take the healthy luxury which nature appoints you, in the rare annual taste of the thing given in those its due days. The vile and gluttonous modern habit of forcing never allows people properly to taste anything. (*Fors Clavigera*, Vol IV)

Cypress trees at Brantwood in the 1890s: five Lawson's Cypress that Ruskin had brought back from Italy line the southern edge of the new Kitchen Garden. They grew to an enormous size before 1980s winds laid them low

In the 1890s six cypress trees that Ruskin had earlier brought back from Italy and planted in the lower garden were moved to form a line on the southern edge of this new Kitchen Garden. These were, in fact, Lawson Cypress (*Chamaecyperis lawsoniana*) rather than the less hardy and more slender true Italian Cypress (*Cupressus sempervirens*). They grew to a great size and became a local landmark until the 1980s when they began to blow over. After a winter storm in early 1991 only one was left and the decision was made to remove it, but not until cuttings had been taken so that the genetic stock of the original trees might be conserved at Brantwood.

Ruskin's additional Kitchen Garden has had to be sacrificed to the car-parking needs of today's many visitors to Brantwood. This would have saddened him deeply, but perhaps he would have taken comfort in the thought that it resulted in the enjoyment of his gardens by so many people. An echo of the Kitchen Garden still survives in the garden below the Café Terrace (see p. 91) and who knows, it may be that the development of a modern interpretation of a kitchen garden for cultivating food and other produce in a sustainable way will become an exciting project for the future.

The Ice House: a visitor emerges from the tunnel leading to the ice chamber

The secret door leading to the underground cistern, fed with water from the Moorland Garden, that helped supply the taps in the house

Ice House

This unusual garden structure deserves a visit before leaving Ruskin's gardens. It represents another of his experiments and is also an example of his concern for others. The Ice House may be discovered by climbing the steps beside Ruskin's cascade (opposite the old front door of the House) and then taking a shady path that curves away to the left. Quickly found, an iron gate guarding the entrance to a rough tunnel in the rock reveals a curving flight of ascending steps cut into the living rock. At the top an opening, with a wooden door, once gave access to the circular ice chamber itself. The opening is situated about half-way between the floor, with its central drain and original slatted oak drainage-decking, and the gently domed roof which has a square central opening to the hillside above, normally covered with a heavy lid of slate. The walls of the elegant interior (4 metres high x 2 metres diameter) curve gently, first outwards and then inwards towards the apex, and are lined with perfect, lime-mortar render. The whole internal space thus has the form and colour of a large, slightly flattened egg-shell standing on end.

It was intended that the structure should be used for the storage of ice, which during the cold winter months of the late nineteenth century could be sawn and collected from the frozen lake. Ruskin hoped that this might then be used during the summer in the Brantwood kitchen and sick-room and be available to local people, especially in times of sickness. Sadly, however, Ruskin relates that the ice stored during the first winter all melted and the Ice House was never again used for its original purpose.

5. JOAN SEVERN

Joan Severn was a most remarkable woman. It has already been noted in passing that in a chapter entitled 'Joanna's Care' in *Praeterita*, Ruskin describes how the seventeen-year-old Joan, or Joanna, Agnew moved from Scotland in 1864 to the Ruskin family home at Denmark Hill, to look after his recently widowed mother. In fact, 'Joanna's Care' also included Ruskin himself, and indeed Joan was destined to continue this caring role for the rest of his life, especially during his declining years at Brantwood. Joan's support of Ruskin at Denmark Hill continued until 1870, during which time he developed a deep attachment to her. In November of that year, however, Joan announced that she had become engaged to be married to a young painter, Arthur Severn, thus threatening both Ruskin's emotional stability and the smooth running of his domestic life. The domestic situation was in part rescued by Ruskin giving the young couple his house at Herne Hill, only a short walk away from Denmark Hill, although the emotional damage remained. Nevertheless, Ruskin's attachment to, and dependence on, Joan continued unabated. When he moved to Brantwood in September 1872 he took Joan and Arthur with him to help arrange the interior of the house, which from then and for the ensuing sixty years became their second home.

During the early years following Ruskin's move to Brantwood he and Joan were regular correspondents, often using the intimate baby language they had developed together at Denmark Hill. Moreover Joan, sometimes alone and sometimes with Arthur and their growing family, frequently travelled north to Brantwood for holidays or for longer periods, to nurse Ruskin through his increasingly frequent bouts of mental and physical illness. Eventually Joan and her family moved there more or less permanently and she took on the role of châtelaine of Brantwood. Relationships were often severely strained, however, with rows and harsh words occurring all too frequently, for Ruskin was irked by his dependence on Joan and her family, and often felt that they were taking over his life and his home, as indeed they were. Joan and Arthur were acutely aware, of course, that their comfortable existence was entirely dependent on Ruskin's goodwill, and perhaps in part for this reason, but also most probably because of Joan's innate kindness and her real affection for Ruskin himself, she stood by him and from 1889 until his death in 1900 nursed him through the long, dark days of his final illness. There is little doubt that Joan could have had Ruskin committed to an asylum at this time, and it is to her very great credit that she did not, and that with the help of a local doctor, George Parsons, she nursed him to the very end.

Opposite: Joan Severn sitting in front of the house at Brantwood. The large-leaved climber against the house wall is no longer there, but may have been a hardy Aristolochia species such as A. macrophylla (Dutchman's Pipe)

Joan Severn's ideas as to what the gardens of a Lakeland country house should be like were very different from those of Ruskin. As Brantwood's châtelaine, she saw the gardens as a combination of family spaces that should be both calming and aesthetically pleasing to Ruskin, herself and the entire Severn family, and as social spaces appropriate to her status in Lakeland society as the 'lady of the house'. She struggled with Ruskin's intellectual approach to everything, not least his gardening activities, and must have found his garden creation schemes during the early Brantwood years extremely trying. Perhaps even then she was planning her own garden schemes for the future.

It has already been emphasised that as Ruskin's life drew to a close in the 1890s he became unable to tend the labour-intensive gardens, paths and steps he had created in the previous two decades. They slowly fell into disuse and became overgrown with weeds. Increasingly, during this decade, Joan Severn stepped in and began to mould the estate to her own very different taste, not by modifying Ruskin's own gardens, which were left in nature's embrace, but by creating entirely new ones of her own. As Collingwood remarks:

> The Brantwood gardens as they now are [in 1903], enlarged and tended by a mistress who loves and understands flowers, and glorified by their charming position on the shores of a mountain lake, are as near the perfect blend of detailed interest and picturesque beauty as anything can be in this northern climate. But they are not Ruskin's gardens. When the first glass-house went up [in the additional kitchen garden, now the car-park], he used to apologise for it to his visitors; it was to please Mrs Severn; it was to grow a few grapes for his friends; he did not believe in hot-houses: and he would take them up the steps he had contrived at the back of the house and point out the tiny wild growths in their crannies, as he led the way to his own private plot.

The Robinson connection

Besides being a talented and imaginative garden maker in her own right, as Collingwood's prose and the evidence of her garden designs testify, Joan Severn was possibly also inspired by William Robinson, the celebrated nineteenth century 'wild-garden maker', with whom she and Ruskin corresponded. Although, like Ruskin, she used wild plants extensively in her gardens, these were not on the whole modest native species, but were usually flamboyant exotics planted principally for colour, scent and dramatic effect. The contrast between Ruskin's approach to wild gardening and that of William Robinson and Joan Severn is evident in letters amongst the Robinson papers at the Lindley Library of the Royal Horticultural Society, London.

Opposite: View from the area of the Brantwood garden that Joan Severn was later to develop as the High Walk. This pencil, ink, watercolour and bodycolour sketch by John Ruskin, dated 1881, looks across the lake to the Coniston fells

74

First, however, it is necessary to quote from *Proserpina*, Ruskin's two-volume work on botany, written while he lived at Brantwood. In Chapter XI, entitled 'On Wildness in Flowers', he wrote:

> I have the following note from Mr. Robinson…in answer to an enquiry of mine about the deadness of colour and vapid smoothness of root of petal in the orange lilies … in my greenhouse: …'There are various lilies allied to the bright orange one of the Piedmontese meadows. To make a fair comparison, you will, of course, be sure that you have the *same* [lily] both in pots and in the garden… It shows remarkable difference between its garden and wild state… Please give us *English* names. "Lilium Fervidum" [a Latin name that Ruskin had invented] is just as much a bar to the fairest gate to knowledge as any other *botanical* name.'

The RHS papers contain the hurriedly written reply Ruskin sent from Brantwood the day after he received Robinson's letter (MS, 5 July 1885):

> So many thanks – but – I can only be sure, in *Proserpina* of the description of the wild flower – <u>you</u> must answer for the potted ones – and I always give Latin as well as English name[s] to every flower I have to name… I never should venture to name at all, if I could not name in Latin.

In contrast Joan Severn wrote, somewhat archly, to Robinson from Brantwood in February 1899:

> I know it is wicked to trouble <u>you</u> — but may any of your officials, on a post card say where I can get "Prunus Pseudo Cerasus" [sic] a double flowering cherry … also if one can buy a Japanese prune [sic] with lovely pale pink double flower?... Forgive my troubling you — ever yours most gratefully.

Although William Robinson was undoubtedly inspired in his creation of aesthetically pleasing wild gardens by Ruskin's drawings and writings about wildness in plants and landscapes, Ruskin's approach to garden making was entirely his own, being concerned principally with studies of the beauty and science of plants for feeding the mind and body and for education, rather than for mere display. In my opinion, if Robinson's influence can be seen anywhere at Brantwood, it is in the gardens created by Joan Severn, although these were equally the result of her own creative abilities, as is abundantly evident in the High Walk and Harbour Walk.

High Walk today, looking towards the lake on a spring day

6. JOAN SEVERN'S GARDENS

High Walk (late 1880s)

As Sally Beamish has remarked:

> the strength of form, simplicity of line and exuberance of colour of the High Walk all reflect the character of Joan Severn.

The view from the High Walk, looking over the Japanese maples (Acer palmatum) *at the bottom of the Maple Walk towards the lake and the Coniston fells. The top of one of the very large* Rhododendron *'Broughtonii' trees just coming into flower is visible to the right of the maples*

Approached from the Painter's Glade, this spectacular yet genteel garden was situated to provide a vista across the lake to the Old Man of Coniston, thereby providing easy access, for those who could not or would not climb higher, to some of the greatest scenery in Lakeland. Sally Beamish continues:

> having been lost for a century amid a growth of young trees and tangled bushes, the re-discovery of this late Victorian viewing terrace in the 1990s changed both the overall character and the balance of Brantwood's gardens, providing an elegant contrast to the wild woodland above and Ruskin's equally wild gardens nearby.

Framed by exotic trees and bordered with beautifully scented old *Rhododendron* (syn. *Azalea*) cultivars and species surrounding a long, narrow lawn, the restored garden now includes an exciting collection of rare shrubs and bold herbaceous plantings to complement the original survivors.

Maple Walk and Cornfield Bank

The Maple Walk leads down from the High Walk to the present-day car-park. The beautiful form and deep red colour of the four, now massive, old Japanese *Acer palmatum* trees on the right towards the end of the path provide a living canopy, supported on arching branches of great architectural impact, and constitute a triumphant final flourish at the end of the southern gardens.

Opposite: The lower end of the Maple Walk, which leads from the High Walk down to the Lower Gardens. The first of the magnificent old Japanese maples (Acer palmatum) *dominates the centre of the photograph, with a large specimen of one of Joan Severn's original, clear yellow flowered* Rhododendron (syn. Azalea) luteum *bushes to the right*

Planted on the rising ground above the path and on the somewhat misleadingly named Cornfield Bank that plunges down from it (the site of a cornfield during Linton's tenure of Brantwood), further rare and interesting shrubs, together with striking herbaceous plantings, provide colour and interest throughout the year.

These plantings include a collection of deciduous, spring flowering Ghent azaleas and several large, clear yellow *Rhododendron* (syn. *Azalea*) *luteum* bushes, survivors of Joan Severn's garden. Also from this period, to the left of the path as one descends, are two venerable old apple trees, currently being rejuvenated, one a Galloway Pippin and the other a Bramley's Seedling. A third apple tree here, of unknown identity, sadly died a few years ago. Lower down there is also the stump of an ancient *Robinia pseudoacacia*, now completely dead, but nevertheless supporting the growth of a rowan sapling that has arisen from a seed dropped by a bird into the broken top of the trunk. And at the lower end of the row of maples and at the very bottom of the Bank is a group of five breathtaking scarlet-flowered *Rhododendron* 'Broughtonii' trees. Similar specimens may be found in the gardens of Muncaster Castle, near Ravenglass, Cumbria, home of the Pennington family for more than eight hundred years. Joan Severn certainly had a link with the family and Sally Beamish has speculated that she may have obtained the rhododendrons from them in the 1880s.

It was clear to Sally Beamish when she began work on the Cornfield Bank that here were the remains of a late Victorian shrubbery, probably originally planted by Joan Severn. She wisely left the original plantings in place, but relocated to the site a collection of modern *Rhododendron* hybrids, planted at various locations in the gardens by Bruce Hanson during his time as General Manager in the 1980s. These bright and beautiful shrubs now provide mature structure and help to screen the car-park from the garden. The rest of the Bank is gradually being replanted, by Sally Beamish, with a mixture of small shrubs, herbaceous perennials and perennial wild flowers to create what she describes as

> a modern interpretation of the late Victorian wild garden style in which native and exotic shrubs and plants are combined in a pleasingly informal way.

The Lower Gardens

Part of this acre of ground formed part of the original kitchen garden of the house and was in use as such as early as the 1850s, although it did not become part of the Brantwood estate until much later. Long before this, however, one of Ruskin's earliest projects at Brantwood was the enlargement and deepening of the harbour, which he completed in 1875. Following the acquisition of the Lower Garden area in 1897 it was first worked on by Joan Severn to create her Harbour Walk, while more recently Sally Beamish and her staff have exploited its potential by creating the Trellis Walk and Hortus Inclusus (see pp. 95 and 100).

Opposite: one of the five scarlet-flowered Rhododendron 'Broughtonii' trees at the bottom of the Cornfield Bank that may have been obtained by Joan Severn from Muncaster Castle

The Harbour Walk with Joan Severn's azalea bushes in full flower, having been 'pruned back to life' by Sally Beamish and her staff

The Harbour Walk (1899) and Daffodil Meadow

The Harbour Walk is now approached through a wooden gate on the opposite side of the road from the car park. Planned by Joan Severn, together with her head gardener Dawson Herdson, to beautify the approach to the harbour (an important point of arrival and departure for visitors to Brantwood), it was completed in 1899, the day that Herdson retired. It takes the form of a simple, curving path with borders on either side. The original plantings included lilacs and scented azaleas (salmon pink and pale gold cultivars of *Azalea mollis* and clear yellow *Rhododendron* [syn. *Azalea*] *luteum*), while the path was edged with Ruskin's favourite spring flower, the headily scented Pheasant's Eye (*Narcissus poeticus*). Joan Severn adored the combination of vibrant colour and heavenly scent, and this Walk down to the lake shore provided both in abundance.

Neglected for nearly a century, the Harbour Walk was restored in 1995. Sally Beamish writes:

> The lilacs had gone, but the old azalea bushes were still there and were pruned back to health. Re-establishing the line of the original path was achieved with the help of an old photograph of Mrs Severn standing in her garden. She was a lady built on generous lines and with her wide Victorian skirt was reckoned to be about 3 foot wide at floor level! Allowing some room for passing, we calculated the old path width to have been about 4 feet. Between the azaleas, where lilacs were, we have planted an unusual selection of herbaceous plants to continue the amazing, blazing splendour of this feature well into the autumn.

Flanking the Walk on one side is a small meadow with early flowering wild daffodils. Originally the plants were probably Lenten Lillies *(Narcissus pseudonarcissus)*, introduced by Ruskin to remind him of happy times at Vevay on Lake Geneva, where this exquisite spring flower bloomed in profusion. Over the years, however, the Lenten Lilies at Brantwood have multiplied and hybridised with local *Narcissus* cultivars and now create a carpet of palest gold every spring.

On the other side of the Harbour Walk is a small orchard, planted by Sally Beamish, and this will be discussed in Chapter 7 (see p. 99).

Opposite: The Harbour Walk in 1911, reproduced from a watercolour by Arthur Severn, R. I., entitled 'Path to the Lake at Brantwood, Lancashire'. Joan Severn's magnificent original plantings of lilacs, cultivars of Azalea mollis *and* Rhododendron *(syn.* Azalea*) luteum and the heavenly scented* Narcissus poeticus *(Pheasant's Eye) are all in full flower*

7. SALLY BEAMISH AND HER GARDENS

In the spirit of John Ruskin

In creating the new gardens at Brantwood, as in the restoration of the Ruskin and Severn gardens and the management of the Woodland and Estate, Sally Beamish has striven to follow what she describes as 'Ruskinian principles'. The most important of these, perhaps, so far as the gardens are concerned, are idealism and open-mindedness – a willingness to embrace new, even challenging, ideas.

In the modern Brantwood, organic practices are used and investigated wherever possible and as resources allow. As interpreted at Brantwood, organic husbandry is a method of management in which the land is regarded as a strong, self-sustaining and vital 'organism', with all the components seen as part of the greater whole. The aim is to create a harmonious environment in which the soil, plants, wild creatures, humanity and landscape are all in tune with one another.

In a small number of areas of the Estate a tentative exploration of 'biodynamic cultivation' is taking place (see Howard Hull's discussion overleaf). This controversial form of land management is based on a series of lectures delivered in 1924 by the German philosopher Rudolph Steiner, at Schloss Koberwitz in Silesia. These were first published in English as *The Agriculture Course* in 1928. The biodynamic gardener recycles wherever possible, and avoids all 'artificial' chemical interventions. Moreover, special organic preparations are made and applied to the soil and plants in minute quantities with the intention of stimulating microbial activity, optimising the composting process and improving soil fertility.

Sally Beamish's interest in exploring differing management regimes like this is more anthropological than scientific. Ruskin's own writings on botany and his garden projects at Brantwood can only be understood by grasping the social and cultural perspective with which he approached them. For instance, the biodynamic gardener believes that the subtle rhythms associated with the sun, the moon, the planets and the stars form the basis of the cultivation, sowing and planting calendar. One is reminded again by this of Ruskin's own reference to the authority of the stars when writing about growing vegetables:

And, for these, your proper observance of season, and of the authority of the stars, is a

Opposite: The Orchard in full bloom – created by Sally Beamish in 1989 for its flowers rather than its fruit, as Ruskin would have wished

vital duty. Every climate gives its vegetable food to its living creatures at the right time; your business is to know that time, and to be prepared for it… (*Fors Clavigera*, Vol IV)

Sally Beamish's intention is that Brantwood should be a rich and varied garden environment, built on sound organic practices, that is at one with its surroundings, as indeed it is.

Secondly, all the new gardens created by Sally Beamish are 'semi-wild', in a Ruskin-like way, with local stone and estate-produced timber being used wherever possible to create the informal hard landscaping.

And finally, each of the new gardens has an educational theme, the visitor being invited and encouraged to learn from the plantings while enjoying their aesthetic qualities.

Sally Beamish scattering 'biodynamic' fluid in the Wildflower Meadow

HOWARD HULL ON BIODYNAMIC STUDIES AT BRANTWOOD

Sally Beamish was first encouraged to consider a Biodynamic approach to Brantwood's estate management by the Ruskin Mill Trust, an organisation that applies Steiner's holistic principles to the education of young people with learning difficulties. I had for some years been exploring the relationship of Ruskin and Steiner's educational thinking in a series of workshops with Andrew Wolpert at Emerson College in Sussex and with Aonghus Gordon at Ruskin Mill in Gloucestershire. By way of this latter connection, Sally contributed a description of Brantwood's gardens and estate to a Biodynamic conference at Freeman College in Sheffield. This pointed up the opportunity for a practical and unprejudiced study with Brantwood's meadow being the 'laboratory'.

Ruskin Mill Trust has supported Sally's Biodynamic studies ever since, providing funding for the Soil Life project in the meadow. The project does not set out to 'prove' the tenets of biodynamics; rather, it takes three areas of land managed under different regimes (Steiner's coming closest to that proposed by Ruskin, but differing in important aspects too) and assesses both the treatments and the results across a spectrum of analytical methods, from scientific soil analysis to Goethian observation. The aim is to understand how, in the long history of husbandry, both valid and misguided ways of 'seeing and doing' arise in every epoch. Like all of Ruskin's own experiments, it goes back to first principles and is a direct response to nature itself. In many ways it is the perspective and culture of the approach that is really under examination, a sort of parable seeking to open our eyes to the wider challenge of configuring our relationship to nature.

A bed of roses

Although arriving by boat is still the very best way to approach Brantwood, the vast majority of visitors today arrive by car and park in the car-park, once, as we have seen, Ruskin's additional Kitchen Garden. To reach the house they then walk through the pedestrian exit at the northern end of the car-park, where Joan Severn's greenhouses once stood. The small but significant bed which rises steeply to the right of this exit has been planted by Ruth Charles with a representative collection of wild and cultivated members of the Rose family (Rosaceae). The rose is said to have been Ruskin's favourite flower and he had studied the members of its family carefully.

Part of Ruskin's affection for the rose may have been in honour of the unattainable love of his life, Rose La Touche, whom he probably first met in 1859, when she was ten years

old. It was not until she was older, however, that his interest in Rose turned into an obsession that was to consume him emotionally until her untimely death in 1875, at the age of only twenty-seven. Even after her death, thoughts of Rose continued to haunt Ruskin for the rest of his life. In 1874 he copied a small group of roses from that part of the petticoat of Spring, in Botticelli's painting *Primavera*, where it is tightly stretched across her thigh, and developed from it a woodcut vignette which he used on the title pages of his later books, including the separate parts of *Proserpina*. Perhaps significantly, in the small watercolour from which the woodcut was derived the roses are painted blue, rather than the pink used by Botticelli. This may have been because Botticelli's painting was uncleaned when Ruskin made his copy and the rose therefore appeared to be blue. However, blue was said to be Ruskin's favourite colour – he always wore a blue stock, for example – and its choice for the roses may also have been made to signify his never-ending quest for the impossible, especially in love.

The family Rosaceae is large and varied, including in its four sub-families trees, shrubs and a great diversity of herbaceous species. It is also a family of immense horticultural importance, some of its members having been cultivated since ancient times. Many of the edible fruits grown in gardens today are members of the Rosaceae, including apple, pear, plum, cherry, almond and strawberry, while the ornamental genera familiar to gardeners include: *Rosa*, *Potentilla*, *Spiraea*, *Chaenomeles*, *Cotoneaster*, *Prunus* and *Alchemilla*. The species and cultivars used in the planting of this small garden bed are listed below.

THE PLANTS TO BE FOUND IN THE ROSACEAE BED NEAR THE CAR PARK PEDESTRIAN EXIT

Spiraeoideae	Maloideae	Prunoideae	Herbaceous
Neillia affinis	*Chaenomeles*	*Prunus tomentosa*	*Sanguisorba menziesii*
Spiraea nipponica	'Pink Lady'	*Prunus laurocerasus*	*Alchemilla conjuncta*
'Snowmound'	*Cotoneaster dammeri*	'Otto Lutyens'	*Aruncus aethusifolius*
Stephanandra incisa	*Cotoneaster* 'Coral		*Potentilla megalantha*
'Crispa'	Beauty'		*Potentilla atrosanguinea*
			Potentilla recta x *warrenii*
			Potentilla nepalensis
			'Miss Wilmott'
			Gillenia trifoliata

Opposite: Rosa rugosa *at Brantwood – a progenitor of the little-known 'Ruskin Rose', a strongly scented double crimson hybrid bred in 1928 by Dr. Walter Van Fleet, physician to the utopian socialist Ruskin Colony in Tennessee*

A grand entrance: the drive

The entrance to the present main drive to the House, formerly the back drive leading to the stables

After leaving the car-park, visitors to the house must walk up the curving 'entrance' drive (originally the back drive leading to the stables). The wide beds on either side of this now important thoroughfare were probably originally laid out by Joan Severn, but when Sally Beamish arrived all that was left of the plantings were some large, clear yellow and occasionally orange azalea bushes, some specimens of the yellow flowered Oregon grape (*Mahonia aquifolium*) and a ground covering of hybrid Solomon's seal (*Polygonatum*). To these she has added a pleasing mix of shrubs such as cultivars of kerria (*Kerria japonica*), silverberry (*Eleagnus* species), dogwood (*Cornus* species), clematis and, to the left of the gate, a single specimen of the delicate, white flowered *Camellia* hybrid 'Cornish Snow'. Between the shrubs are carefully placed groups of herbaceous perennial cultivars such as *Aquilegia*, *Omphalodes*, *Helleborus* and *Dicentra*, and large clumps of the wiry yet delicate yellow flowered *Epimedium*. In late summer, plants of *Dactilicapnos (Dicentra) macrocapnos*, a spectacular scrambling relative of Bleeding Heart (*Dicentra spectabilis*), cover the azaleas above the drive with a profusion of pendant yellow flower trusses.

Close to the house, on the right of the path as one approaches the door, are six small, faux stone troughs – in fact recycled sinks – planted to represent different mountain habitats: acid woodland, well drained woodland, tufa rock crevice, acid rock crevice, acid scree and limestone scree (see below for details). The whole effect is harmonious and peaceful, giving visitors a welcoming sense of arrival at a place that is rather special but not in the least degree grand or intimidating.

PLANTS GROWING IN THE SIX HABITAT-THEMED TROUGHS AT THE TOP OF THE DRIVE
LISTED IN ORDER FROM THE TOP OF THE DRIVE

1. Acid Woodland	2. Well Drained Woodland	3. Acid Rock Crevice
Hepatica nobilis	*Polygala chamaebuxus* 'Grandiflora'	*Genista pilosa* var. *minor*
Salix myrtilloides 'Pink Tassels'	*Hepatica nobilis albiflora*	*Saxifraga oppositifolia* 'Splendens'
Primula elatior	*Vaccinium chaetothrix*	*Saxifraga × lincolni-fosteri* 'Diana'
Soldanella villosa		*Saxifraga stribrnyi*
		Antennaria dioica 'Minima'

4. Tufa Rock Crevice	5. Acid Scree	6. Limestone Scree
Armeria juniperifolia (dark-flowered)	*Geranium sessiliflorum* subsp. *novae-zelandiae* 'Nigricans'	*Saxifraga paniculata* 'Rosea'
Dianthus 'Eileen Lever'	*Eriogonum caespitosum*	*Primula frondosa*
Saxifraga 'Tycho Brahe' (*× doerfleri*) encrusted saxifrage	*Saxifraga* 'Boston Spa' (*× elisabethae*)	*Primula marginata*

'Jumping Jenny', Ruskin's personal boat named after Nanty Ewart's brig in Redgauntlet, *was built to his specifications by his secretary, Laurence Hilliard. In this photograph, taken during the summer of 1891, probably by Lund of Coniston, a bearded Ruskin has taken the oars while Joan Severn is seated in the stern and a standing Arthur Severn looks on from an adjacent boat*

Food for thought: the Café Terrace

Upon arrival at or departure from Brantwood, most visitors find an excuse to visit the Jumping Jenny café-restaurant situated in the old Stables and named after Ruskin's rowing boat, built to his own design. Beside the café is the old Coach House, housing the woodman's workshop, Ruskin's coach and the original Jumping Jenny.

Hardy visitors, opting to sit at the tables on the terrace rather than by the wood-burning stove in the cosy café interior, are rewarded with a fine panorama of the lake and fells and, on the bank below, a close-up view of a delightful small garden planned by Ruth Charles. This is divided into three cultivated terraces planted with an eclectic mix of culinary herbs, vegetables and flowering annual and perennial herbaceous species and cultivars, evoking Ruskin's own garden experiments. Growing against the old iron fence between the garden and the Café Terrace are old northern varieties of apple, grafted on to dwarfing rootstocks and espalier-trained so as not to spoil the view.

ESPALIER APPLES GROWING ALONG THE FENCE OF THE CAFÉ TERRACE LISTED FROM GATE

*Bradley's Beauty*** Cooking/dual purpose apple, newly discovered in the South Lakes and originally found growing on the Witherslack Mosses

*Proctor's Seedling** Dessert apple that originated in Lancashire and was known in 1934.

Yorkshire Beauty (syn. Greenup's Pippin) * Dual purpose apple found in the garden of shoemaker Greenup, in Keswick, in the late eighteenth century.

*Mrs Lakeman's Seedling** Dual purpose apple raised at Stockfields, Northumberland, in 1900.

* Based on information from the catalogue of the National Fruit Collection, University of Reading, England.
** Based on information published by the North Cumbria Orchard Group.

The Fern Garden (1991)

This extensive collection of over 200 British native fern varieties illustrates some of the many different forms that this ancient plant group may take. Work began on this garden in 1991 to commemorate the hundredth anniversary visit to Brantwood of the British Pteridological Society, founded in the Lake District in 1891. It also pays homage to W. J. Linton, Ruskin's predecessor at Brantwood, for this fascinating and talented man was an energetic amateur botanist who wrote and illustrated the first Cumbrian fern flora in 1865. Sally Beamish writes of the creation of the Fern Garden as follows:

> It seemed appropriate that Linton's work should be honoured beside that of Ruskin, and so ferns described in *The Ferns of the English Lake Country* were planted above the house, in an area that had become choked with *Rhododendron ponticum*. Unwrapping the site from its dense evergreen cover revealed the remnants of some paths that traversed the hillside, and left a clean but hungry soil exposed. The surfacing

Opposite: Fern or moss? This exquisite small watercolour by John Ruskin has been known for many years as 'Ferns on a Rock, Brantwood 1879'. The tiny plant depicted may possibly be a loosely drawn, attenuated Dryopteris fern species, precariously rooted on the damp surface of a stone, but could be a fern-like moss. Whichever it may be, its identity has so far baffled the fern and moss experts the author has consulted

93

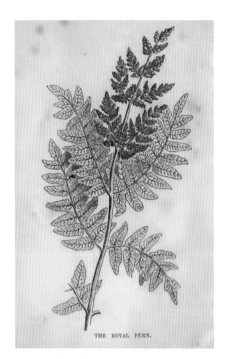

THE ROYAL FERN.

The Royal Fern (Osmunda regalis), *frontispiece of* Ferns of the English Lake Country – With a List of Varieties, *written and beautifully illustrated by W. J. Linton while at Brantwood and published in 1865. Magnificent specimens of the Royal Fern have been planted around John Ruskin's Pond (see p. 59), while one of the beds in Sally Beamish's Fern Garden is devoted to specimens illustrated in Linton's book*

bedrock was exploited as a potential home for crevice-lovers and great heaps of leaf-mould added to satisfy the incoming ferns.

Begged, borrowed and bought, the fern collection began to grow, including a fine specimen of Royal Fern *(Osmunda regalis)*, from a garden in Eskdale Green, that was three feet tall with its roots and well over 100 years old. The creation of this garden provided us with an excellent opportunity to learn to overcome the problems of moving large and heavy items through inaccessible areas using applied maths, physics and a fair amount of grunting – an excellent combination of techniques!

The ferns are arranged in a series of scattered beds that blend into the landscape. The main informal groups of ferns represented are listed below, although the boundaries between groups have become blurred because the spores of individual species spread around in the wet climate of Brantwood.

INFORMAL GROUPS OF BRITISH FERNS IN THE FERN GARDEN

Polypodies (*Polypodium vulgare* – common polypody; and related forms) and blechnums (*Blechnum spicant* – hard fern; and related forms)

Males and scaly males (*Dryopteris filix-mas* – male fern, *D. affinis* – scaly male fern; and related forms)

Bucklers (*Dryopteris cristata* – crested buckler fern; and related forms)

Shield ferns (*Polystichum aculeatum*- hard shield fern; and related forms)

Lady ferns (*Athyrium filix-femina* – lady fern; and related forms)

Rock and crag ferns (e.g. *Asplenium ruta-muraria* – wall-rue, *Asplenium trichomanes* – maidenhair spleenwort; and other species found growing on rocks and crags)

SPECIES LISTED IN *FERNS OF THE ENGLISH LAKE COUNTRY* BY W. J. LINTON,

The Linton Fern Bed Species from the Coniston Valley		Ferns elsewhere in the Fern Garden Species from other parts of the 'Lake Country'	
Athyrium filix-femina	lady fern	*Asplenium scolopendrium*	hart's tongue fern
Blechnum spicant	hard fern	*Cystopteris fragilis*	brittle bladder fern
Dryopteris aemula	hay-scented buckler	*Gymnocarpium robertianum*	limestone oak fern
Dryopteris affinis	scaly male fern	*Polystichum aculeatum*	hard shield fern
Dryopteris dilatata	boad buckler fern	*Polystichum lonchitis*	holly fern
Dryopteris filix-mas	male fern	*Polystichum setiferum*	soft shield fern
Gymnocarpium dryopteris	oak fern		
Osmunda regalis	royal fern		
Phegopteris connectilis	beech fern		
Polypodium vulgare	common polypody		

The Trellis Walk (1988)

Originally part of the Kitchen Garden, the Trellis Walk was created in 1988 as part of the Lower Gardens complex to provide an attractive alternative to the then derelict Harbour Walk for visitors arriving at Brantwood by water. After climbing the steps from the jetty, one may reach the house, therefore, either by going straight ahead to the Harbour Walk or by turning sharp left into the Trellis Walk and following it as it then turns right and takes one towards the main road and the house. On each side of the path the long, narrow beds are divided into sections by trellis screens. The linear form of the Walk and the natural exuberance of the growth of plants at Brantwood made this a particularly challenging garden to create and maintain. Sally Beamish writes:

> It began as a sequence of traditional herbaceous borders, planted only for colour and interest. Later, and until recently, it was developed to play a more significant role in the language of Brantwood's gardens, by providing an opportunity for the visitor to explore the role of plants in the history of our changing culture. Nine trellised enclosures were created, and in them vignettes of nine different cultural epochs were planted to demonstrate the variety of ways in which plants have assisted and inspired artists, architects, craftsmen and designers over the centuries. The sequence started with the Medieval Physic garden and progressed via the New World, Georgian classical design and the High Victorian ball-gown, embellished with living flowers, to the Arts and Crafts Movement and the exuberant elegance of Art Nouveau. Then followed the utilitarian needs of two World Wars and the contrasting extravagance of 'Flower Power', the sequence ending with the contemporary role of plants in the twenty-first century.

Significant investment in time and labour was required to maintain such complex plantings within confined spaces, and eventually it was decided, therefore, to replant the Trellis Walk. This has provided an opportunity to develop a new concept for the garden, and the one chosen is an interpretation of a recurring theme in Ruskin's writings, that of 'challenging the accepted', as encapsulated in his fascinating work on botany, *Proserpina*. The name chosen by Ruskin for this, his only major work on plants, was the name of an ancient Roman goddess, the daughter of Ceres, goddess of agriculture and crops, and Jupiter, god of sky and thunder. Proserpina's story forms the basis of the myth of Springtime and her name, appropriately, derives from the Latin *prospere*, to emerge, as in the germination of a grain of wheat.

Proserpina was first published as a series of ten pamphlets, the first appearing in 1875,

The Trellis Walk at its best. Designed by Sally Beamish in 1988, the maintenance of this exuberant garden required significant time and labour. It is currently being redesigned to explore a Ruskinian theme, 'challenging the accepted'

three years after Ruskin moved to Brantwood, and the last in 1886. All were illustrated with wonderful engravings and woodcuts of plants and flowers, executed by George Allen, Ruskin's publisher, and Arthur Burgess, and based on Ruskin's own paintings and drawings, some of them merely sketches. Many of the illustrations are undoubtedly of plants growing in the gardens at Brantwood or in the surrounding countryside. The ten pamphlets were later brought together by George Allen into two volumes, the first published in 1882 and the second in 1888.

Ruskin despised the writings of conventional botanists and says that the writing of *Proserpina* was undertaken to:

> put… some elements of the science of botany into a form more tenable by the ordinary human and childish faculties… to make the paths of approach to it more pleasant.

The bulk of the book is a highly controversial (indeed, many would say, misguided) attempt to devise a new, non-Linnaean taxonomy of plants based on aesthetic principles rather than scientific analysis and understanding. Throughout *Proserpina* plants are given human minds and personalities and the Divine purpose is frequently referred to. Although controversial, the book most certainly invites the reader to look at plants in new ways and, as illustrated in Chapter 3 above, contains passages of great beauty and of botanical insight. Above all, however, *Proserpina* is testimony to John Ruskin's thirst for knowledge and understanding of plants, his acute powers of scientific observation and his very considerable skill as a botanical artist and illustrator. Using Ruskin's revolutionary thoughts to inform the planting and interpretation of the Trellis Walk will be a challenge for Sally Beamish, but she will, no doubt, rise to it as she has risen to the many and varied challenges that have confronted her since her arrival at Brantwood some twenty-five years ago. She says that in *Proserpina*:

> Ruskin was taking his readers with him on a journey of the mind into an unknown and, for him, unresolved world of plants.

Perhaps this statement gives a clue as to how the new garden might develop.

Opposite: Acanthoid Leaves, 1879, by John Ruskin. These two pencil and brown ink working botanical drawing of 'two different aspects of the same leaf' on overlapping sheets may have been made at Brantwood. They are of marsh thistle (Cirsium palustre) and were intended as part of an illustration in Proserpina. *Ruskin describes there how 'the thistle leaves are full of complex and sharp sinuosities, and set with intensely sharp spines passing into hairs, which require many kinds of execution with the fine point to imitate it all'*

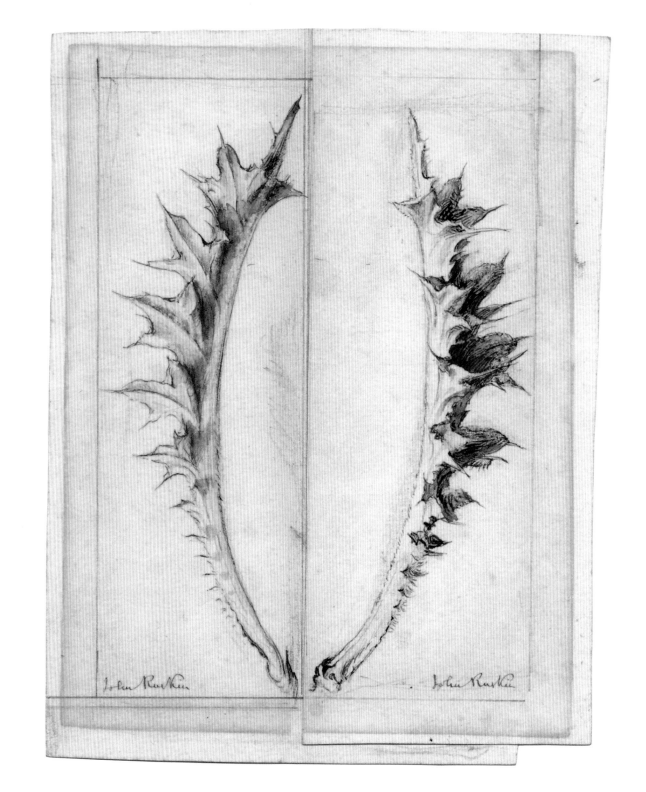

John Ruskin

John Ruskin

Orchard (1989)

Enclosed by the Trellis Walk and the Harbour Walk is a small orchard, planted in 1989 for its flowers rather than for its fruit, as Ruskin would have wished. The trees are all old cultivars, the king of the orchard being Keswick Codlin, first found near Ulverston in 1793. It produces beautifully golden fruits that are equally delicious as eaters or cookers. This and the other cultivars, whose blossoms present a glorious sight in spring, are listed below.

APPLE CULTIVARS PLANTED IN THE ORCHARD*.

Beauty of Bath   Dessert apple that originated at Bailbrook, Bath, Somerset. Introduced into commerce, c.1864.

Court Pendu Plat   Dessert apple that originated in mainland Europe, was first described in 1613, but is thought to be much older. Sometimes called 'The Wise Apple' because it flowers late, thereby escaping frost damage. It is known by many different synonyms across Europe.

Edward VII   Cooking apple first recorded in 1902 and introduced into commerce in Worcester in 1908.

Egremont Russet   Dessert apple, English, first recorded in 1872 and now widely grown commercially.

Grenadier   Cooking apple, first recorded in 1862 and introduced into commerce in c.1875.

Keswick Codlin   Culinary apple found growing on a rubbish heap at Gleaston Castle, near Ulverston in Lancashire. It was first recorded in 1793.

Ribston Pippin   Dessert apple, raised at Ribston Hall, Yorkshire, from seed brought from Rouen, France and planted in c. 1707.

* Based on information from the catalogue of the National Fruit Collection, University of Reading, England

Opposite: A magnificent specimen of Keswick Codlin. Its beautiful golden fruits (right) were popular with Victorian gardeners as the first cookers of the season. The bright colours of the azaleas in the Harbour Walk may be seen through the rustic fence beyond the tree

Hortus Inclusus (2000)

The Latin phrase *hortus inclusus* means, quite simply, 'an enclosed garden'. This garden form has been used from the very earliest times, but especially during the medieval period, when the concept of an enclosed garden was linked to the 'purity' of the Virgin Mary. The phrase was also used as the title of a collection of Ruskin's letters to his friend Susanna Beever, who lived at The Thwaite, on the opposite side of the lake, and provided him with his great stone Seat (see p. 53).

The Hortus Inclusus at Brantwood is indeed a 'secret garden', completely enclosed by walls and fences, and may only be entered through a small wooden gate that can easily be missed, on the left of the Trellis Walk as one approaches the house. It was completed in 2000, and since it once formed part of Brantwood's original kitchen garden it was planted with the many native British herbs used throughout the centuries for cooking, to provide sweet aromas, to beautify the home or in traditional medicine. The 180 species originally planted in the garden were arranged by natural habitat, practical and aesthetic use, and season.

Sally Beamish writes of its development:

Hortus Inclusus, a secret garden, in which the beds are based on the shape of the dining room windows at Brantwood and are planted with native British herbs. This photograph was taken in the garden's heyday, before opportunistic and planted perennials became a problem

> Dropping about 18 feet vertically from the top to bottom, this garden employs a series of terraces to level the slope. The Gothic design of Ruskin's dining room window provided inspiration for its shape and the estate provided the green-oak timbers for its construction. Traditional woodworking techniques have been used throughout and neither nail nor screw has been required. The rounded sections of timberwork were taken from naturally curving boughs.

> At Brantwood we aim to explore the creative possibilities of many local raw materials, and in Hortus Inclusus copper and slate have been used to make attractive labels and containers, whilst wood, stone and wool have been used for construction and decoration in a variety of ways.

> The garden was designed as a garden for learning and follows the Ruskinian principles of education, promoting vivid experience, sharp observation, the making of connections, and contemplation.

Over the years both opportunistic and some planted perennials have become a problem in this garden, calling to mind Ruskin's own description of a weed in *Proserpina,* 'thrusting

Ruskin's dining room windows at Brantwood, the inspiration for the shape of the beds of Hortus Inclusus

itself where it has no business, and hinders other people's business' (see p. 40). The most difficult to cope with is tufted vetch *(Vicia cracca)*; other challenging plants are creeping cinquefoil *(Potentilla reptans)*, hedge bedstraw *(Gallium mollugo)* and hedge woundwort *(Stachys sylvatica)*; and these are in addition to the usual garden perennial invasives such as docks *(Rumex species)* and ground elder *(Aegopodium podagraria)*. Hand weeding and even in desperation the use of chemical herbicides, despite the commitment of the staff to organic horticultural practices, have all proved inadequate, so the beds have recently been excavated and a light-excluding membrane inserted below soil level to suppress the weeds. This will undoubtedly be effective, given time, but in the interim, so that the garden retains its message and special charm, the herbs that can cope with restriction of their roots have been replanted in clay pots half buried in the soil. Meanwhile, in the borders that frame this garden, the battle continues.

Volunteers hand scything the Brantwood Wildflower Meadow in readiness for the outdoor theatre

Wildflower meadow

Beyond the Hortus Inclusus, sloping gently up from the lake shore to the road, is a great hay meadow, regularly grazed by cattle and a small herd of Lakeland sheep and where Sally Beamish's elderly horse, Sam, may sometimes be seen grazing peacefully. When Howard Hull arrived as director of Brantwood, in 1996, this was simply a conventionally managed piece of grazing land comprising mainly grass, with few wild flowers. With Hull's encouragement, however, Sally Beamish ceased applying chemical fertilizers and other additives to the meadow and replaced them with dressings of farmyard manure. She also carefully adjusted the management and grazing regimes to promote the proliferation of wild flowers amongst the grass. Stock was excluded from early May onwards and grazing was not resumed until after the meadow was mown at the end of July or early August, the exact date depending on the weather. A small area of the meadow is now hand-mown by a team of volunteer scythers, to accommodate the outdoor theatre which is a regular feature of the Brantwood summer season, the remainder being cut with machinery by a local farmer who, after turning the hay to facilitate drying, bales it and removes it for the winter feeding of his stock.

Gradually the wild flowers have returned and the diversity of grasses has increased (see

The Wildflower Meadow in full bloom. Visible in the foreground is a single purple flower head of heath spotted orchid, the yellow flowers of meadow buttercup, the small white flowers of eyebright and the seed heads of yellow rattle. The two latter species are partially parasitic on the grasses and help to prevent them dominating the meadow flora

the list below), seed for the incoming species presumably coming in part from the natural seed-bank in the soil, thus reflecting the flora of the meadow in the distant past, and partly as a result of dispersal from elsewhere by birds, other animals and wind. Especially important has been the establishment of hemi-parasitic plants such as yellow rattle (*Rhinanthus minor*) and eyebright (*Euphrasia officinalis*), which attach themselves to the roots of the grasses and extract nutrients from them, thereby reducing their vigour and thus their ability to out-compete the wild flowers. Now that the meadow is once again rich with flowering species, it not only dons its floristic coat of many colours every summer, but also attracts a great diversity of bees, butterflies and other insects that, in turn, attract the many birds and other animals that feed on them.

The meadow is a great success story, giving a glimpse of the beauty of the flower-rich Lakeland hay meadows of a previous age, before modern farming methods were introduced. A future project for the garden staff will be to develop ways of providing visitor access to the meadow at peak flowering time, but in such a way as to conserve the fragile soil structure and the vulnerable wildflower and meadow grass populations.

WILDFLOWER MEADOW FLORA

Wild flowers

autumn hawkbit *Leontodon autumnalis*
bird's-foot-trefoil *Lotus corniculatus*
buttercup, bulbous *Ranunculus bulbosus*
buttercup, meadow *Ranunculus acris*
common knapweed *Centaurea nigra*
eyebright *Euphrasia officinalis*
great burnet *Sanguisorba officinalis*
heath spotted orchid *Dactylorhiza maculate*
pignut *Conopodium majus*
red clover *Trifolium pratense*
ribwort plantain *Plantago lanceolata*
yellow rattle *Rhinanthus minor*

Meadow grasses

cock's foot *Dactylis glomerata*
common bent *Agrostis tenuis*
crested dog's tail *Cynosurus cristatus*
meadow fox-tail *Alopecurus pratensis*
perennial rye grass *Lolium perenne*
red fescue *Festuca rubra*
rough stalked meadow grass *Poa trivialis*
smooth meadow grass *Poa pratensis*
sweet vernal grass *Anthoxanthum odoratum*
Yorkshire fog *Holcus lanatus*

Geological specimens on a specimen cabinet in Ruskin's study: wood engraving from the Library Edition of Ruskin's Works

Mountain Garden (2008)

It is perhaps appropriate to end with geology, and local mountain plants, the former a subject close to Ruskin's heart throughout his life. According to his father, John James, he had been 'an artist from childhood but a geologist from infancy'. Indeed, his father may well have initiated and encouraged this interest when he brought home a collection of fifty minerals purchased for five shillings from a geologist in the Lake District; copper ore from Coniston, garnets from Borrowdale and Bristol 'diamonds' (transparent rock crystal found in Clifton limestone) were among his treasures. He valued his stones for their individual beauty, for their distinguishing characteristics and for the way they invited close examination.

Ruskin began a mineralogical dictionary at the age of twelve and it is said that his first ambition was to become as famous as the President of the Geological Society, who was then Charles Lyell (1797-1875), the foremost geologist of his day, author of *Principles of Geology* and forward-thinking and influential friend of Charles Darwin. From collecting and classifying, Ruskin progressed to studying broader aspects of geology and in his (somewhat random) collection of geological studies, *Deucalion: Collected Studies of the Lapse of Waves, and Life of Stones* (1879), he wrote:

> No subsequent passion has had so much influence on my life.

The Mountain Garden at Brantwood, created to celebrate this lifelong love of geology, is situated at the side of the house that faces the lake, and has three principal elements, as follows.

Alpine Bank   The delicate plantings of saxifrages and other alpines such as cyclamen, gentian and rock-rose, on the slope above the path, all reflect Ruskin's affection for the Alps, the Scottish Highlands and other mountainous areas that inspired so many of his writings and drawings.

Crystals   Ruskin's passion for geology and seeing every stone as a mountain in miniature is celebrated in the collection of crystals – many of them to be found in the local fells – displayed in slate boxes beside the path. Even the boxes themselves have been given the form of some of the more common crystalline shapes: cubes and regular polygons. Around the boxes the plantings are designed to create the textural effects of the vegetation on the Coniston fells.

Local Fell Plants   Ruskin urged people to look closely at their surroundings and the detail of the individual objects that make up the bigger whole. The small area below the path is, therefore, planted with species that grow wild on the fells about Coniston, and thus provides an opportunity for the visitor to examine and enjoy, close-up, the exquisite beauty of the plants that clothe the larger landscape of the fell-sides across the lake.

Beyond the Mountain Garden the path leads through a small woodland planting for winter and early spring interest, now called the Front Garden (see list on p. 117). It leads the visitor to what was the original main gateway and drive to Ruskin's garden and house, an old and stately lime marking the place. Visitors in Ruskin's day would have walked or ridden up the drive, passing the cascade (see p. 67) on the way to the old front door – a fitting place to end this garden tour.

View of Brantwood from the bottom of the original main drive, with a lady in white near the house, and a view of the lane and the lake to the right

8. ENVOI

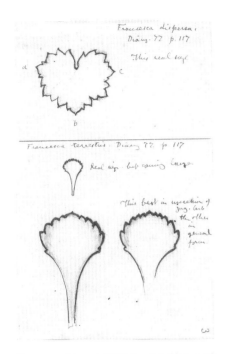

'Francesca dispersa', 1877. Pencil and brown ink drawings by John Ruskin depicting the leaves of two species or hybrids of Saxifraga, a genus, renamed by Ruskin, that includes London Pride

Opposite: Fronds of bracken (Pteridium aquilinum) turning golden brown on the woodland floor following the first cold nights of autumn. Probably our commonest fern, bracken spreads by means of underground stems (rhizomes), rapidly establishing dense stands, to the virtual exclusion of other plants. The dead fronds, which soon turn coppery brown, persist for the entire winter

The policies of Brantwood constitute a unique garden landscape or, perhaps more accurately, a group of unique gardens within a magical woodland landscape, for they cannot be regarded as a 'landscape garden' in any conventional sense. This is but one of the many reasons why, once visited, Brantwood draws one in and enters one's soul. But what other qualities make the place so special? Perhaps the most important is that every visit becomes a journey, not a mere physical journey, but a journey of the mind, in which a sense of adventure and discovery is ever present. Often, when one passes another visitor on a path leading through the woodland from one garden to another, the sparkle of expectation, of being on an exciting quest, is immediately apparent in their eyes, as it must be in one's own.

In the preceding pages I have presented the gardens, with some minor deviations, in the order in which I 'discovered' their individual secrets and came to appreciate them myself, rather than according to any strict chronological criteria. There are groupings, certainly, based on the three creative but very different people who brought them into being – John Ruskin, Joan Severn and Sally Beamish – but even these follow my own journey of discovery, which began with Ruskin.

I had been studying Ruskin's flower drawings in the collection of the Ruskin Library in Lancaster University and felt that I might better understand their enigmatic beauty if I visited the home and gardens of the man who had made them, to see the place where so many of his delicate subjects actually grew. Chance took me first to the Professor's Garden and I was rewarded on my way there by the sight of saxifrages – relatives of London Pride – growing around and between the steps leading up to it. I was immediately able to put names to a page of simple, thumbnail-sized drawings labelled, in Ruskin's hand, *'Francesca dispersa'* and *'Francesca terrestris'*. These had been puzzling me, for no scale was given, nor any indication of what the flowers might be like, and search as I might the genus *Francesca* could not be found in any Flora or other work of botanical or horticultural reference on my bookshelves. But here were the plants themselves, in Ruskin's garden, and the names were clearly his own invention, as *Proserpina*, his audaciously unconventional botanical work, would reveal to me later:

The second tribe, (at present Saxifraga) growing for the most part wild on rock, may,

I trust, even in Protestant botany, be renamed Francesca, after St. Francis of Assisi; not only for its modesty and love of mountain gravel, and poverty of colour and leaf; but also because the chief element of its decoration, seen close, will be found in spots or stigmata.

I was hooked, and so my own journey of discovery began.

Contemplation of the Professor's Garden gave me a much deeper appreciation of Ruskin's concern for the needs of less privileged working men and women, encapsulated in *Unto This Last* and explored more extensively in *Fors Clavigera – Letters to the Workmen and Labourers of Great Britain*. The mix of beautiful flowers and shrubs with vegetables and herbs reminded me of the ideals of the Arts and Crafts movement, which he inspired, where beauty and utility were combined, each feeding off the other. This was no simple cottager's kitchen garden, but a garden to feed the mind and the spirit, as well as the body, of the labourer.

The exquisite natural detail and simple elegance of the woodland beyond the Professor's Garden, and the serene beauty of the nearby Painter's Glade, with its distant views of the lake, the fells and the sky, brought me perhaps a little closer to an understanding of Ruskin's view that the primary concern of art should be the accurate documentation of nature, a central tenet of his great work of art criticism, *Modern Painters,* and an approach, he argued, that enabled J. M. W. Turner to develop an increasingly profound insight into the portrayal of natural forces and atmospheric effects. The Painter's Glade also emphasised for me Ruskin's love of early Italian painting, for the woodland about it is, as Collingwood tells us, reminiscent of the background of a work by Botticelli. And who but Ruskin would see the potential visual beauty in something as prosaic as a tennis court?

At first sight Zig-zaggy, the Purgatorial Mount, was an enigma. Yes, I could see what Ruskin was trying to achieve structurally – both a three-dimensional representation of part of Dante Alighieri's great work of literature and a practical experiment in gardening on a steep hillside, as Italian farmers do. I could not, however, reconcile the plantings with those in his other gardens. It was only when I properly appreciated that this was a truly hybrid garden – Ruskin's landscape design combined with Sally Beamish's imaginative planting to interpret his ideas for a modern audience – that it came alive for me.

My 'discovery' of the Moorland Garden came much later, later even than my exploration of Joan Severn's gardens, so in that sense it is a garden out of sequence in the text. It was winter, the garden structure laid bare, with no attempt having been made by the Brantwood staff, deliberately and wisely, to recreate or reinterpret the moorland plantings. For the first time I could feel the presence of the restless, questing mind of its creator: always exploring and communicating new concepts, often several at a time; always aiming for an impossible ideal; always combining utility with beauty; and always reluctant to let go, even in old age and infirmity. There was something else too, a man fizzing with innovative, even revolutionary, ideas who all too often lacked the practical skills and knowledge to bring them to successful fruition. I had the same sad sense of lost opportunities when I subsequently visited the Pond and the Ice House, and when I read Ruskin's own accounts of his 'waterworks schemes' in *Praeterita*, his autobiography.

It was only gradually that I came fully to appreciate Joan Severn's remarkable gardens. To begin with, in my mind, these were simply glistering gilt on Ruskin's gingerbread. Slowly it became clear to me that they gave a remarkable insight into their creator's personality. Like her they were larger than life, as expressed most strikingly in the exuberance of the High Walk and Harbour Walk, both overflowing with colour and scent. There was a generosity of spirit there too, a love of life and also, perhaps, a visually compelling reaction to Ruskin's strictly intellectual approach to every project he embarked on. Finally, they seemed to be an important expression of the way Joan Severn wished to be perceived by Lakeland society, as the 'lady of the big house' at Brantwood.

It was through her gardens too that I came to appreciate the caring side of Joan Severn's personality. True to her kindly, surrogate mother relationship with Ruskin, she did not seek to rival his creations while he still had strength to work on them. And when that strength ebbed away, she did not attempt to modify or destroy his work, but left it to be quietly reclaimed by nature, while making her own gardens elsewhere at Brantwood.

What a triumph Joan Severn's gardens are! Her talents as an imaginative and inventive garden maker in the 'wild style' espoused and popularised in the late nineteenth century by William Robinson are abundantly evident in all her work.

And as my appreciation of the gardens of Ruskin and Joan Severn grew and developed, so too did my admiration for Sally Beamish, Head Gardener. Howard Hull, General Manager at Brantwood, and his predecessor, Bruce Hanson, had the generosity and wisdom to give her the intellectual and managerial space and the physical and financial resources to develop her ideas, supported in no small measure by her dedicated and skilled staff and many volunteer helpers. Sally Beamish's gardens are imaginative and ambitious in their exploration of ideas and ideals, just as Ruskin's were, as is evident from her accounts of the making of the Fern Garden and the design of the Trellis Walk.

It is in the restoration and replanting of the Ruskin and Joan Severn gardens, however, that her finest achievements may be seen. With immense sensitivity she has restored their structure, so far as is necessary and possible, and has carefully conserved and rejuvenated any plantings that remained. With great tact she has not attempted to replant the Moorland Garden, allowing the spirit of its creator to shine through, even on the coldest and wettest of days. Elsewhere, with the 'good manners' that can only stem from deep empathy, she has complemented Ruskin's and Joan Severn's plantings with entirely fresh material of her own.

The result of this careful work is not a collection of dusty museum showcase gardens dedicated to the memory of two long-dead people, but a series of living gardens, set in actively managed, working woodland, all reinterpreting the ideas and personalities they embody for a very large, modern audience of visitors, and continually evolving. The work of Sally Beamish and her staff and volunteer helpers in the management of the woodland and gardens is the glue that binds the Brantwood garden landscape together, unifying it, perhaps for the first time in its history.

Finally, it is important to emphasise that although this garden landscape is certainly very important, it is definitely not grand or exclusive: it is complex, conceptually and structurally, but completely accessible to all, as Ruskin would have wished; it is managed, yet brings one as close to the world of nature as any wilderness I know. It is a landscape for thinkers, for dreamers and for those who simply love plants for their own sake – a landscape for every woman and every man and for children of all ages. It is one of the treasures of Lakeland. Do visit it, time and time again if you can, as I do, and I hope that, to paraphrase some lines from T. S. Eliot's *Four Quartets*, the end of all our exploring will be to arrive where we started and know it for the first time.

Opposite: The Daffodil Meadow in full bloom. It was planted at the very end of Ruskin's life to remind him of his former travels in Europe, and in it his spirit lives on

the least graceful of all corollas I know being merely
a tube cut into five lobes, of which one is torn down
with great straggling stamens the curly
of it is its great point—

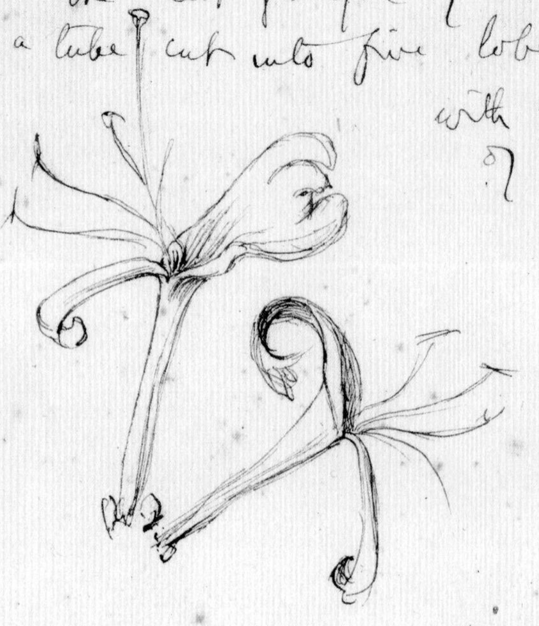

they grow from small calices
and green — with incipient
and scales between

in a ragged bunch
something picone like
but not indeed

this corolla performs
function of calyx
shutting up like a bell
quite but at the mouth

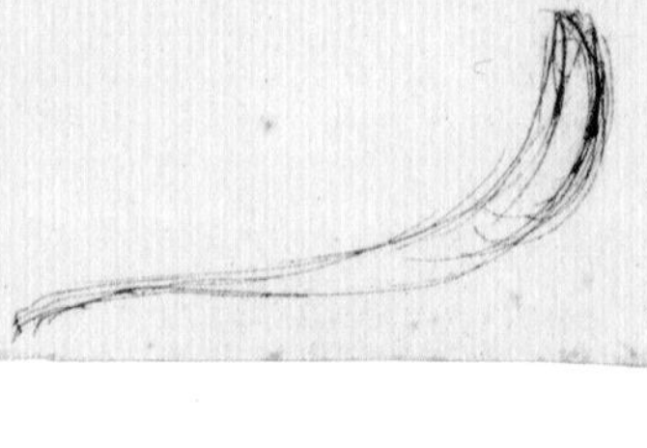

Ruskin, John, eds. Cook, E. T. and Wedderburn, Alexander, *The Works of John Ruskin*, ('Library Edition'), George Allen, London, and Longmans, Green & Co. New York, (1903–1912.
  (A searchable database is available from the website of the Ruskin Library and Research Centre, Lancaster University).
  Principally consulted were:
  The Poetry of Architecture (Vol. 1);
  Modern Painters (Vols. 3-7);
  Unto This Last, etc. (Vol. 17);
  Loves Meinie and *Proserpina* (Vol. 25);
  Deucalion and Other Studies in Rocks and Stones (Vol. 26);
  Fors Clavigera (Vols. 27-29);
  Praeterita (Vol. 35);
  The Letters of John Ruskin, Vols. I and II (Vols. 36-37).

John Ruskin's letters to Joan Severn (1864 to c.1895); Notebooks and Worksheets; Diaries (various dates 1835 to 1888), The Ruskin Library and Research Centre, Lancaster University, Lancaster

Ruskin, John, ed. O'Gorman, Francis, *Praeterita*, OUP, Oxford, 1978

Ruskin, John, ed. Wilmer, Clive, *Unto This Last and Other Writings*, Penguin, London, 1997

Batchelor, John, *John Ruskin: No Wealth But Life*, Random House, London, 2001

Beamish, Sally et al, *The Lower Gardens, Brantwood* (informal, short leaflet guide); *Brantwood Gardens Pictorial Map* (single sheet map); *Estate Walk: with Sally Beamish, Head Gardener* (informal, short leaflet guide); *A Pictorial Guide to the Ferns of Brantwood* (coloured leaflet); *Brantwood: John Ruskins Gardens – a guide to the Walks & Gardens at Brantwood* (brief leaflet guide); *Brantwood garden story-boards*; *EU Grant Application*, The Brantwood Trust, Coniston, 1992-2013

Bisgrove, Richard, *William Robinson: The Wild Gardener*, Frances Lincoln, Ltd, London, 2008

Blamey, M., Fitter, R. and Fitter, A., *Wild flowers of Britain and Ireland*, A & C Black, London, 2003

Brickell, C. ed., *The Royal Horticultural Society A-Z Encyclopedia of Garden Plants*, Dorling Kindersley, London, 2008

Collingwood, W. G., *Ruskin Relics*, Isbister & Co. Ltd, London, 1903

Collingwood, W. G., 'The Ancient Ironworks of Coniston Lake', *Historical Society of Lancashire and Cheshire Transactions*, Vol. 53, pp. 1–22, 1901

Collingwood, W. G. *The Book of Coniston*, 3rd edition. Titus Wilson, Kendal, 1906

Collingwood, W. G., *Lake District History*, Titus Wilson, Kendal, 1925

Dearden, James S., *John Ruskin: A Life in Pictures*. Sheffield Academic Press, Sheffield, 1999

Dearden, James S., *Brantwood: The story of John Ruskin's Coniston home*. The Ruskin Foundation, Coniston, 2009

Hanson, Bruce, *Brantwood: John Ruskin's home 1872-1900*, The Brantwood Trust, Coniston, 1994

Helmreich, A. L., 'Re-presenting Nature: Ideology,

Art, and Science in William Robinson's *Wild Garden*' in: *Nature and Ideology – Natural Garden Design in the Twentieth Century* (Joachim Wolschke-Bulmahn, ed.). Dumbarton Oaks Research Library and Collection, Washington, D.C., 1997

Hunt, John Dixon, *The Wider Sea: A Life of John Ruskin*. J. M. Dent & Sons Ltd, London, 1982

Hilton, Tim, *John Ruskin: The Early Years 1819-1859*, Yale University Press, New Haven and London, 1985; *John Ruskin: The Later Years*, Yale University Press, New Haven and London, 2000

Holme, C. ed., *The Gardens of England in the Northern Counties*, The Studio Ltd., London, 1911

Ingram, David and Wildman, Stephen, *Ruskin's Flora: The Botanical Drawings of John Ruskin*. Ruskin Library and Research Centre, Lancaster University, Lancaster, 2011

Jackson, Kevin, *The Worlds of John Ruskin*, Pallas Athene, London, in collaboration with The Ruskin Foundation, Coniston, 2010 and 2014

Linton, W. J. (1865). *Ferns of the English Lake Country: With a List of Varieties*. Hamilton, Adams & Co, London, 1865, 2nd ed. J. Garnett, Windermere, 1878

Linton, W. J., *Memories*. Lawrence and Bullen, London, 1895

Longville, Tim, *Gardens of the Lake District*. Frances Lincoln, Ltd, London, 2007

Loynes, Fiona, *The Historical Context of Brantwood and Ruskin at Brantwood*. Unpublished manuscript (Cat no. T120), Ruskin Library, Lancaster University, Lancaster, (date unknown)

Mabberley, D. J., *Mabberley's Plant Book*. CUP, Cambridge, 2008.

Steiner, Rudolph, *Agriculture: A Course of Lectures Held at Koberwitz, Silesia, June 7 to June 16, 1924*; English edition Bio-Dynamic Farming & Gardening Association, Inc., 1993

Opposite A working botanical drawing of honeysuckle flowers (Lonicera periclymenum) by Ruskin. The drawing is not dated, but it could have been based on observations made at Brantwood, for honeysuckle occurs throughout the woodland. The notes in brown ink, in Ruskin's hand, begin: 'Honesuckle The least graceful of all corolla I know being merely a tube cut into five lobes, of which one is torn down…'

PLANTS TO LOOK OUT FOR AT BRANTWOOD ARRANGED BY GARDEN AND SEASON
COMPILED BY SALLY BEAMISH AND RUTH CHARLES

	SPRING	SUMMER	AUTUMN	WINTER
PROFESSOR'S GARDEN	*Ranunculus aconitifolius* *Anemone nemorosa* *Helleborus × hybridus* Lenten rose *Geranium sylvaticum* 'Mayflower'	*Hydrangea serrata* 'Grayswood' *Iris chrysographes* 'Black Knight' *Rosa* 'The Garland' *Rosa gallica* var. *officinalis* *Ligularia przewalskii* *Potentilla thurberi* 'Monarch's Velvet' *Fuchsia* 'Hawkshead'	*Rodgersia podophylla* *Geranium* 'Ann Folkard'	*Cedrus deodara* *Griselinia littoralis*
ZIG-ZAGGY	*Pyrus communis* 'Black Worcester' *Gunnera magellanica* *Hosta sieboldiana* var. *elegans* plantain lily	*Euphorbia mellifera* honey spurge *Crambe maritima* sea kale *Celmisia semicordata* *Diplarrena moraea* *Hemerocallis* 'Pink Damask' *Camassia cusickii* *Rheum palmatum atropurpureum* ornamental rhubarb	*Stipa gigantea* *Crocosmia masoniorum* *Hesperantha coccinea* 'Major' *Pyracantha* 'Dart's Red' *Hakonechloa macra* 'Aureola' *Molinia caerulea* 'Transparent' *Datisca cannabina* *Dipsacus fullonum* teasel *Eryngium agavifolium*	*Corokia cotoneaster* *Ophiopogon planiscapus* 'Nigrescens' *Pyracantha* 'Dart's Red' *Rubus cockburnianus*
HIGH WALK	*Lamprocapnos* (*Dicentra*) *spectabilis* bleeding heart *Pieris formosa* *Lamium orvala* *Polygonatum × hybridum* Solomon's seal *Chaenomeles japonica* Japanese quince *Rhododendron luteum* Himalayan honeysuckle *Rhododendron* (*Azalea*) *mollis* seedlings *Primula wilsonii* var. *anisodora*	*Paeonia delavayi* *Crinodendron hookerianum* Chilean lantern tree *Rhododendron augustinii* hybrid *Telekia speciosa* heart-leaf oxeye *Osmunda regalis* royal fern *Lobelia bridgesii* *Astilbe* 'Midnight Arrow' *Euphorbia griffithii* 'Dixter' *Hemerocallis* 'Golden Chimes' *Ligularia przewalskii* *Primula florindae* *Meconopsis* 'Lingholm' *Francoa sonchifolia* bridal wreath	*Blechnum chilense* Chilean fard fern *Dactylocapnos* (*Dicentra*) *macrocapnos* *Astilbe* 'Fanal' *Sorbus aucuparia* form *Crateagus × prunifolia*	

Opposite Brantwood from the other side of Coniston Water

115

	SPRING	SUMMER	AUTUMN	WINTER

HARBOUR WALK	*Rhododendron (Azalea) mollis*
	Rhododendron luteum
	  Himalayan honeysuckle
	Crocus 'Whitwell purple'
	Narcissus poeticus
	  pheasant's eye
	Narcissus pseudonarcissus vars.
	  Lenten lily
	Galanthus nivalis and *G.n.* 'Flore
	  Pleno' snowdrops
	Lilium pyrenaicum
		Hemerocallis 'Timothy' day lily
		Hemerocallis fulva 'Green
		  Kwanso' Dutch lily
		Rosa 'Félicité Perpétué'
		Dierama pulcherrimum angel's
		  fishing rod
		Dierama igneum
		Lilium henryi
		Lilium 'La Toya'
		Lilium 'Nove Cento'
			Crocosmia 'Dusky Maiden'
			Crocosmia 'Severn Sunrise'
			Crocosmia 'Golden Fleece'	

TRELLIS WALK
This area is currently being re-developed. Only the plants likely to be retained are listed
	Clematis montana
	Clematis montana var. *rubens*
	Clematis montana var. *grandi-*
	  flora
	Pulmonaria officinalis
	Geranium phaeum
	Geranium sylvaticum 'Mayflower'
	Rosmarinus officinalis
	
	Matteuccia struthiopteris
		Humulus lupulus 'Aureus'
		Lonicera periclymenum 'Belgica'
		Lonicera japonica 'Halliana'
		Rosa gallica var. *officinalis*
		Rosa 'Pink Perpétué'
		Rosa 'Zéphirine Drouhin'
		Paeonia officinalis 'Rubra Plena'
		Rosmarinus officinalis
		Origanum vulgare 'Aureum'
		Acanthus spinosus
		Acanthus mollis
		Cynara cardunculus
		Cirsium rivulare
		  'Atropurpureum'
		Aruncus dioicus
		Iris chrysographes 'Black Knight'
		Hosta fortunei var. *aureo-*
		  marginata
		Hosta 'Royal Standard'
		Penstemon 'Andenken' and
		  'Friedrich Hahn'
		Rodgersia pinnata
		Rodgersia podophylla
		Foeniculum vulgare
		Matteuccia struthiopteris
			Clematis tangutica
			Buddleia × *weyeriana* 'Sungold'
			Morina longifolia
			Helianthus 'Lemon Queen'
			
			Cynara cardunculus
			
			Foeniculum vulgare
			Matteuccia struthiopteris
				Rosmarinus officinalis

116

	SPRING	SUMMER	AUTUMN	WINTER

HORTUS INCLUSUS	*Convallaria majalis*
	   lily-of-the-valley
	Aquilegia vulgaris
	   granny's bonnets
	Galium odoratum
	   sweet woodruff
	Polemonium caeruleum
	   Jacob's ladder
	Primula vulgaris primrose
	Primula veris cowslip
	Primula elatior oxlip
		Viburnum opulus
		   guelder rose
		Persicaria bistorta 'Superba'
		   bistort
		Artemisia absinthium
		   wormwood
		Lilium martagon
		Athyrium filix-femina
		   'Minutissimum'
		Verbascum nigrum
		   black mullein
		Filipendula vulgaris
		   dropwort
		Myrrhis odorata
		   sweet cicely
		Polemonium 'Hopleys'
			Viburnum opulus
			   'Xanthocarpum'
			Stachys officinalis betony
			Aconitum napellus
			   monkshood
			Euonymus alatus 'Compactus'
			   winged spindle bush
			Origanum vulgare
			   wild marjoram
			Succisa pratensis
			   devil's bit scabious
				Clematis vitalba
				   traveller's joy
				Buxus sempervirens box
				Arum italicum subsp.
				   italicum 'Marmoratum'
				   cuckoo pint

MOUNTAIN GARDEN	*Pulsatilla vulgaris*
	   pasque flower
	Primula elatior oxlip
	Salix lanata woolly willow
	Primula auricula
	Saxifraga species and cultivars
		Origanum vulgare
		   'Compactum'
		Helianthemum nummularium
		   common rock rose
		Hieracium lanatum
		   woolly hawkweed
		Alchemilla alpina
		   Alpine lady's mantle
			Fagus sylvatica 'Asplenifolia'
			   cut-leaved beech
			Cyclamen hederifolium	

	Erinus alpinus fairy foxglove
	Dianthus deltoides maiden pink
		Myrica gale bog myrtle
		Dactylorhiza fuchsii
		   common spotted orchid
		Luzula nivea
		   snowy woodrush
			Woodsia silvensis	

FRONT GARDEN	*Helleborus* × *hybridus* seedlings
	   Lenten rose
	Blechnum penna-marina
	Primula vulgaris primrose
	Pachyphragma macrophyllum
	Omphalodes verna
	   blue-eyed Mary
		Potentilla rupestris
		Athyrium filix-femina 'Frizelliae'
		   tatting fern
			Bupleurum longifolium	*Viburnum bodnantense* 'Dawn'
				Ilex cornuta × *pernyi* 'Drace'
				Viburnum tinus 'Eve Price'
				Rubus tricolor

	SPRING	SUMMER	AUTUMN	WINTER

HOUSE ENVIRONS	*Pieris* 'Forest Flame'
	Ribes sanguineum
	  flowering currant
	Rhododendron niveum
	Amelanchier lamarckii
	  snowy mespilus
	Erythronium dens-canis
	  dog's-tooth violet
	Erythronium 'White Beauty'
	Erythronium 'Pagoda'
	Crocus 'Ruby Giant'
	Cornus mas
	  cornelian cherry
	Camellia 'Cornish Snow'
	Camellia 'Inspiration'
	Rhododendron yakushimanum
	  hybrid
	Primula prolifera
		Eucryphia x *nymansensis*
		  'Nymansay'
		Corokia x *virgata*
		Primula wilsonii var. *anisodora*
		Chaerophyllum hirsutum
		  'Roseum' pink hairy chervil
		Buddleia 'Lochinch'
		  butterfly bush
		Phlomis fruticosa
		  Jerusalem sage
		Geranium 'Rozanne'
		Dierama pulcherrimum
		  angel's fishing rod
		Nepeta 'Six Hills Giant'
		  catmint
			Vitis vinifera 'Purpurea'
			Vitis 'Brant'
			Vitis coignetiae
			Ficus 'Brown Turkey'	

CORNFIELD BANK	*Azalea* (Ghent hybrid)
	Rhododendron 'Grandeur
	  Triomphante'
	Malus domestica 'Galloway
	  Pippin'
	Rhododendron x *williamsii*
	Rhododendron 'Broughtonii'
	Dryopteris erythrosora
	Enkianthus campanulatus
	  inkberry
	Camellia x *williamsii* 'St Ewe'
	Berberis darwinii
	Chaenomeles japonica
	  Japanese quince
	Polystichum setiferum
	  'Divisilobum'
	Athyrium niponicum var. *pictum*
	  Japanese painted lady fern
	Spiraea 'Arguta' bridal wreath
	Lamprocapnos (Dicentra)
	  spectabilis 'Alba'
	  bleeding heart
	Rhododendron x *williamsianum*
		Geranium psilostemon
		
		Dryopteris erythrosora
		Euphorbia griffithii 'Fireglow'
		Rhododendron 'Winsome'
		Geranium 'Orion'
		Francoa sonchifolia
		  bridal wreath
		Salvia forsskaolii
		Polemonium 'Hopeleys'
		Kirengeshoma palmata
		Verbascum phoeniceum
			Eupatorium cannibinum
			  hemp agrimony
			Anemone x *hybrida* forms
			Anemone hupehensis
			  'Splendens'
			Anemone hupehensis
			  'September Charm'
			Dryopteris erythrosora
			Enkianthus campanulatus
			  inkberry
			Hydrangea serrata 'Tiara'
			Acer palmatum seedlings
			Geranium 'Orion'
				Dryopteris erythrosora
				
				Polystichum setiferum
				  soft shield fern

Estate Trail

3

Path Closed

7

5

4

Northern
Gardens

6

16

8

Brantwood
House

Southern
Gardens

2

15

9

1

14

12

Lodge

Coach
House

13

11 Car Park

10

KEY

● Seating   Easy gradient/few steps
- - Moderate gradients/steps   ▪▪▪ Steep gradients/steps

1 Mountain Garden   12 Zig-Zaggy
2 Fern Garden & Ice House   13 Jumping Jenny Restaurant
3 Moorland Garden   14 Coach House Loft
4 Professor's Garden   15 Linton Building
5 Ruskin's Seat   16 Studio
6 Painter's Glade   17 Trellis Walk
7 Ruskin's Pond   18 Harbour Walk
8 High Walk   19 Hortus Inclusus
9 Maple Walk   20 Ruskin's Harbour
10 Garden Exit   21 Jetty and Boats
11 Southern Garden Entrance

17

18

Lower
Gardens

19

20

21

The Gardens at Brantwood: Evolution of Ruskin's Lakeland paradise, by David Ingram

First edition 2014

ISBN 978 1 84368 099 4

Published by Pallas Athene, Studio 11B, Archway Studios, 25-27 Bickerton Road, London N19 5JT, in collaboration with the Ruskin Foundation

© 2014 David Ingram

The right of David Ingram to be identified as the author of this work is hereby asserted

Half title: View from the High Walk in the heart of the gardens looking across the lake to the Coniston Fells (Chapter 6)

The author and publisher would like to thank the following for the use of their photographs: cover and on pp. 4, 6, 81 by and courtesy of Nina Claridge; half title and p. 14 by and courtesy of Val Corbett; pp. 9, 106 by and courtesy of Brian Sherwin; pp. 16, 19, 36, 37, 39, 40, 41, 44, 48, 50, 60, 61, 67, 68, 72, 75, 87, 91, 92, 97, 104, 105, 107, 112 courtesy of the Ruskin Foundation (Ruskin Library, Lancaster University); pp. 20, 21, 31, 42, 57, 59 (top), 62 (bottom), 64, 65, 70, (71 top), 75, 79, 88, 94, 100, 101, 119 courtesy of the Brantwood Trust; pp. 26 (top), 26 (bottom), 30, 45, 82, 86, 95, 102, 103 by and courtesy of Howard Hull; pp. 32, 51, 58, 98 by and courtesy of Ruth and David Charles; p. 38 courtesy of the Lakeland Arts Trust (Abbot Hall Art Gallery, Kendal, Cumbria); p. 76 courtesy of James Dearden; p. 99 by Su Haselton, courtesy of Northwest Ecological Trust, Lydiate, Merseyside; p. 114 by and courtesy of Fred Mason; p. 120 map by Robert Henfrey and the Brantwood Trust

Photographs on pp. 2, 10, 23, 24, 27, 28, 29 (top), 29 (bottom), 35, 43, 46, 49, 52 (top), 52 (bottom), 54, 56, 59 (bottom), 62 (top), 63, 66, 69, 71 (bottom), 77, 78, 83, 84, 90, 93, 111 by David Ingram

Printed in England by Park Lane Press on fully recycled and carbon-neutral paper, using fully sustainable, vegetable oil-based inks, power from 100% renewable resources and waterless printing technology. Print production systems are registered to ISO 14001: 2004, ISO 9001: 2008 and EMAS standards, and all site carbon emissions are offset through The Rainforest Concern Charity via their Forest Credits scheme.